Create Your Home in Counted Thread

This simple little cottage with its honeysuckle-covered porch has been set in a flower-filled garden. The cottage is worked mainly in tent stitch with shaded cashmere stitch to represent the old tiles of the roof and upright cross stitch for the band of ornamental tiles. The chimneys and base of the porch are worked in pattern darning. The flowers have been worked freely with a variety of straight stitches and French knots, but tent stitch has been used as a base throughout. The background has been worked entirely in tent stitch with a single strand of thread to suggest distance.

Create Your Home in Counted Thread

Mary Jenkins

David and Charles

For my husband Peter. Thank you for all your
support and encouragement in everything I do.

Keep cleane your Samplers, sleepe not as you sit,
For sluggishness doth spoile the rarest wit.

From A Booke of Curious and Strange Inventions,
called the first part of Needleworkes, published in 1596.

A DAVID & CHARLES BOOK
David & Charles is a subsidiary of F+W (UK) Ltd.,
an F+W Publications Inc. company

First published in the UK in 1996 as *House and Garden Samplers*
First paperback edition 2005

Distributed in North America
by F+W Publications, Inc.
4700 East Galbraith Road
Cincinnati, OH 45236
1-800-289-0963

A catalogue record for this book is available from the British Library.

ISBN 0 7153 1943 4

Typeset by Tony Hadland, National Museums & Galleries of Wales
Printed in China by SNP Leefung
for David & Charles
Brunel House   Newton Abbot   Devon

Visit our website at www.davidandcharles.co.uk

David & Charles books are available from all good bookshops; alternatively you can contact our
Orderline on (0)1626 334555 or write to us at FREEPOST EX2 110, David & Charles Direct,
Newton Abbot, TQ12 4ZZ (no stamp required UK mainland).

Contents

Introduction

House and garden samplers have always been one of the most visually appealing and sought after types of embroidery. An old sampler with an attractive house and garden, surrounded by trees, flanked with flower-filled pots and attendant animals, attracts collectors who are prepared to pay high prices for good examples.

When we study such a sampler we may fondly imagine that the house depicted is the stitcher's own, with her pets lovingly portrayed. This is rarely the case. Usually the house was a pattern selected or drawn by the teacher and copied by her pupils. This is why the same house can appear on many samplers. There may have been variations between the pupils' work but whether this is due to individual design choices is open to question.

Many of us would like to embroider our own home, but are not inspired by the building in which we live – we may live in a flat and dream of a cottage. Why should we not sew our dream house? In reality it might be uncomfortable to live in but as a picture it can fulfil a fantasy. Your garden can have flowers all year round with all your favourites blooming at the same time.

House and Garden Samplers gives stitchers all the information they need to develop samplers designed around their own houses and gardens or to recreate favourite dreams. Chapter by chapter I will explain how to design and stitch your own sampler. All the elements which give this style of embroidery its charm and interest are included. You have a choice: you can chart your own house, or embroider one of the houses in this book.

The majority of the houses featured are based on British vernacular architecture which is attractive and challenging because it has such great variety. It encourages the use of many different stitches to depict its various textures. There are also examples of more modern houses to show what can be achieved with a needle. If you live in other parts of the world you can adapt the techniques to suit your local style of house building.

The style of samplers featured is based on that of old eighteenth- and nineteenth-century samplers that we now admire. It is possible to retain the traditional design using the same elements. We can still have our animals and flower borders, but give the sampler an updated look. We can draw on the past but make it an embroidery of the present day. Any house can make an interesting embroidery, all that is needed is a little imagination and know-how.

————————

This sampler by Elizabeth Lyons dated 1839 has all the ingredients that we associate with the word 'sampler'. You can clearly see three distinct divisions in its format, and its themes are typical of the nineteenth century, with Adam and Eve a major feature. Here the house is placed at the base rather than in the middle of the sampler, as I prefer. Such a grand house might well have had a park surrounding it, represented here with deer and a few trees, rather than a garden. It also has some unusual features: the eagles, the bunch of 'carrots' and a lady- could it be Elizabeth herself, emerging from the house?

CHAPTER ONE

Inspired by the Past

SAMPLERS worked long ago have a tremendous appeal for present-day stitchers, providing a glimpse into a past world. Now we, the needlewomen of today, must play our part by producing samplers as a legacy portraying our life and reflecting all the many facets of the late twentieth century. It is a responsible job as a sampler sewn now may become part of a museum collection in the future. By stitching one we are forging a link in the chain, joining the past with the future.

THE FIRST SAMPLERS

Old samplers are the most written about forms of early textiles and even people who know nothing of embroidery can usually recognize one. So many were sewn and they have survived in such large numbers that many families may still own one.

An alphabet, verse, a house with trees, large flowers in pots, animals, some figures (maybe Adam and Eve), all surrounded by a formal flower border – these are the popular elements that give this textile folk art its charm; but this type of sampler, though sought after now and widely collected, is only one of the many differing forms of the sampler.

The earliest-known samplers were collections of patterns and trial pieces for other forms of embroidery, but although they were referred to constantly in early literature as familiar and cherished objects, we do not know what they looked like as no one thought to describe them. A sampler by Jane Bostocke dated 1598, which can be seen in the Victoria and Albert Museum, was the first one found to be named and dated. However, as it is almost square in shape, it is not typical of the samplers that immediately followed it or that might have been its undated contemporary.

During the late sixteenth and early seventeenth centuries, samplers played an essential role in a gentlewoman's life. Needlework was an important pastime and the embroiderer used her sampler as we would a book of favourite stitches; it was her record and *aide-mémoire*. At first glance these samplers look rather mundane: some were pieces of linen scattered with a variety of motifs known as 'spots', others were very long and narrow with bands of either coloured counted thread patterns or self-coloured cutwork and lace techniques. Sometimes these spots and bands were combined on one piece of work. These early samplers were not meant to be displayed but were thought to have been rolled and stored in the workbox, to be referred to when the needlewoman was looking for ideas, as we would refer to a pattern book today.

In the mid-seventeenth century the decorative aspect of embroidery was fulfilled by the fashion for needlework pictures, caskets, mirror frames and other related items. The band and spot samplers were thought to have been worked either at the same time as practice pieces or as a prelude to working these very elaborate items. Certainly some

of the patterns used on decorative items are to be found on the samplers. These embroideries, some of which were worked on fine linen in canvaswork stitches and others in stumpwork and beadwork techniques, used the same design sources as the woven tapestries of the period. Just as today we make cushions to match our curtains so the needlewomen of the seventeenth century used the themes from the tapestries that hung on their walls for smaller items to decorate their homes. The designs were taken from the early pattern books and books of engravings and have classical and biblical themes. It is thought that they were drawn by professional draughtsmen for the young women to sew; however, it is their stitched interpretation that is so delightful. The people, animals, flowers,

MARY HALE 1838

This sampler by Mary Hale has the most delightful house which is so lovingly stitched it would be nice to think that it belonged to the little girl who embroidered it. We could almost imagine it to be her Wendy house. It looks rather like an example of the cottage orné which were built towards the end of the eighteenth and early nineteenth centuries, but in reality it was probably a pattern chosen for Mary to stitch by her teacher.

Although the house and grounds, surrounded by an elaborate border, are charming, the colours are rather sombre and are typical of those used on so many samplers at this time. Because of this, one almost does not notice the awful spotted animal chasing the stag across the park. The rather jolly sheep are also completely ignoring the dreadful scene behind them.

birds and insects are shown in a humorous and carefree way, and because they were copied directly from pattern books, paying no account to scale and perspective, this adds to their charm. While tent stitch was the basic stitch used, other stitches such as rococo, Hungarian and cushion were added to create interest and texture. Many shades of the same colour were built up to give depth and richness to the work, and as all were worked on such fine linen they must be viewed through a magnifying glass to be appreciated.

Samplers, then, were a working tool and, because they were not meant to be decorative, they do not have an immediate visual appeal for us. We need to study them closely to understand their purpose, examining the stitches and techniques. The workmanship is usually exquisite and if viewed through a magnifying glass you can fully appreciate their beauty. A great many stitches were recorded on samplers; the average needlewoman's repertoire is said to have extended to forty stitches. However the construction of some of these stitches and how they were worked has been lost, and, though some are still to be found in our books today, they are perhaps not distinctive enough to persuade modern-day embroiderers that they can add something to their work.

Though preserving a stitch is a worthy aim, it has to prove itself worthwhile. I find that when students practise a stitch their interest is marginal until they see how it has been used before on an old embroidery – then they are fired with enthusiasm. The link has been made when they can see the stitch enhancing their work. Only then does its use and preservation make sense to them. When practising stitches, think how you can use them in your work. We should not simply copy old samplers but use the knowledge gained from them in a constructive way to add another dimension to the samplers we are sewing today.

BAND SAMPLER

Working a reproduction band sampler is a way of immersing yourself in and understanding the patterns and stitches on old samplers and it can be compulsive. It was worked purely as an exercise but once interest is kindled in this type of sampler it is very difficult to stop at one, as there are so many patterns you can record.

Most museums have band and spot samplers for you to study and there is a wonderful collection formed by Dr Douglas Goodhart, donated by him to the National Trust and housed at Montacute House in Somerset. These early samplers, once thought to be rather dull, are now the most valuable of all and command very high prices when sold.

THE CHANGING SAMPLER

It is difficult to know when and why samplers stopped being used as substitute pattern books and became a picture worked in the schoolroom. One theory is that they became more and more elaborate, incorporating lace and cutwork techniques which made them so fragile that they were difficult to roll and store. Another is that the elaborate patterns collected for use on clothing simply became out-dated when fashions decreed simpler forms of embroidery.

Whatever the reason, in the early eighteenth century the sampler became a product of the schoolroom. Its layout was altered: its shape changed to that of a picture; the motifs and bands remained the same but instead of random patterns dotted around they were placed in a design; verses and alphabets were now important elements; and, eventually, by around 1760 houses appeared. Now that the sampler had become a picture to be worked by young children, fewer stitches were used, and unfortunately this trend continued until later only cross stitch was used.

There was now a strata of society with money and with social pretensions. It became the thing to do to educate your daughters and girls were sent to private schools where an important part of their education was the stitching of a sampler. Being a good needlewoman was something to be proud of, and the finished sampler hanging on the wall in the parlour was comparable to the present-day framed certificate, advertising to everyone that the parents could afford to educate their daughter. Every school had its own sampler design, usually chosen by the teacher who probably relied heavily on the pattern books now available to her. While very little was original, every teacher had her own favourite motifs and her own ways of sewing them. The layout of the sampler was decided upon and closely supervised by the teacher giving little scope for originality. Often the only enlivening factor of the

schoolroom samplers are the mistakes that the little girls made, although these were probably a minor tragedy at the time.

F.G. Payne, writing about samplers for the National Museum of Wales in 1939, says:

From an examination of any large collection of samplers one is forced to conclude that while their workers may have evolved an original motif sometimes and occasionally recorded their own houses, gardens, pets etc, they more frequently copied from illustration of patterns current over a wide area. It is sometimes difficult to detect new features: the thatched cottage on a sampler dated 1772 might be taken as a reflection of some contemporary feeling for the picturesque were it not for the similar piece of rusticity on a Stuart embroidery. Many apparent innovations are found on examination to be simply reappearances.

It is disappointing to face up to the fact that the houses depicted in early samplers were not the actual homes of the little girls who stitched them, but unfortunately this would seem on the whole to be true. There is a much photographed sampler in the Victoria and Albert Museum sewn by Sophia Stephens which bears the name Horse Hill House, near London. It is dated 183– (Sophia probably unpicked the last number at some time to hide her age!). We might assume that Sophia was stitching her own home. The very same house, however, this time with no name but surrounded by an identical border and motifs, appears on a smaller sampler by Eleanor Roberts dated 1835 (see page 14). Whose house was it? Perhaps it was the school and Sophia gave it the name of her own house. Recently, I discovered another sampler hung in Thomas Hardy's birthplace in Dorset (now owned by the National Trust) which surely must have the same source. It has the same date, layout, border, motifs etc, but the house is slightly different and this time is called Newton Cottage. The mystery deepens. The study of old samplers is a fascinating and frustrating occupation. You can help to avoid such confusion in the future. When you embroider your house, name it and add the address, the postal code and telephone number if there is room. Alternatively write all these details on a piece of paper with any other information you think may be of interest, such as your reason for sewing it, and frame this

behind the sampler. Think of the surprise it will be for the fortunate owner in years to come and what a help for future historians.

From the mid-eighteenth to the mid-nineteenth century samplers continued to be a product of the schoolroom but the materials used deteriorated and cross stitch was almost the only stitch used. Schools were no longer the domain of the wealthy few, and more children were receiving some form of education. As well as the Seminaries for Young Ladies, there were charity schools, orphan schools, board schools, Sunday schools, dame schools, and all taught some form of sampler making.

While there is no doubt that the very early samplers demonstrated a high point in needlework and were true certificates of excellence, and that the exercise of sewing samplers slowly deteriorated through the centuries to become stereotyped and almost mass produced, we must not forget that each sampler, whatever the quality, represents many hours of work which only those of us who sew can understand and appreciate. We must not be intimidated by the perfection of the early samplers: their makers had an expertise with the needle that few of us can achieve today for they did very little else except embroider. The samplers worked in the schools, however, were certainly not perfect, and their mistakes are only too apparent. Just look at the corners – you will very rarely find four that match. But it is the struggle that the student had with their subject that gives them such appeal: the lopsided corners, the often deformed Adam and Eve, the angel with the rather cross expression. We can understand their striving; we can relate to their failed attempts at perfection, and we can take comfort that the mistakes they made then add to the samplers' charm now.

SEVENTEENTH-CENTURY NEEDLEWORK PICTURE
This picture of a lady in contemporary costume holding a rose, depicts one of the senses, in this case smell. She is surrounded by animals, birds and insects, with a castle in the background, and this is a typical and delightful example of its kind. The picture is in wonderful condition, the colours are clear and unfaded, and is one of many in an outstanding collection housed in The Burrell Collection, Glasgow. A border such as this could be worked today using favourite flowers and pets.

ELEANOR ROBERTS 1835

This sampler has the same house and many of the motifs as one by Sophia Stephens in the collection of the Victoria and Albert Museum. Sophia has unpicked part of the date on her sampler and leaves only 183- recorded. However, she has identified the house as

Horse Hill House near London. Her sampler is bigger with many more motifs but it is undeniably from the same source. There are probably many other samplers with the same house. Could it have been the school house?

CHAPTER TWO

Planning a Sampler

YOU may already have worked a needlecraft kit and be familiar with a sampler chart. These professional charts are very good value as all the design decisions have been made for you and the colours already chosen. You know exactly how the design will turn out as you have a picture of the finished product to inspire you. However, after completing one or more such kits you may want to design your own personal record.

If you feel nervous about designing – and most of us do at first – it is a good idea to base your first attempt on something already made. It could be a chart already in your possession from which you could retain the border and the verse, but change the house and add different animals. This could be your starting point and would help to give you confidence.

EQUIPMENT FOR DESIGNING

If you do decide to take the plunge and draw up your own sampler chart you will need the following equipment:

2 sheets of size A3 graph paper

Graph paper of the same scale on which to draw motifs and lettering

Paper for sketching

Ruler, eraser, HB pencils and sharpener

Felt-tip pen suitable for graphic work, ie drawing fine lines fluently – not all fine pens do this

Glue stick, Blu-Tack and adhesive tape

Paper scissors

Tracing paper

SAMPLER PLAN

On page 16 there is a basic sampler design plan which I have found very reliable in the past. If you follow the instructions and use this format for your design you will create an embroidery the same size as Rose Lodge (page 18).

If you study old samplers you will find that many can be divided into three distinct sections which are, from the top:

1 Lettering – alphabets and/or verse
2 Main element – very often a house but always something large
3 Plants, animals and birds

These sections may appear in a different order but the three divisions are usually there. This gives us a very useful format on which to base our new samplers. It is perfect for:

1 Verse
2 House
3 Garden with animals

These separate bands need not be of equal size – it will depend on how much room you need to express your ideas. The divisions need not be apparent on the finished sampler. They are there to help you at the design stage.

All the house designs in this book fit this basic sampler plan and the suggested verses, animals and borders are in proportion, to this plan. However, if you want to design your own house, garden and other motifs, you will find that more detailed help is provided later on in the book, particularly in Chapter Five.

EACH SQUARE = 10 SMALL SQUARES ON GRAPH PAPER. NOTE: Adapt size of sections to fit your house design.

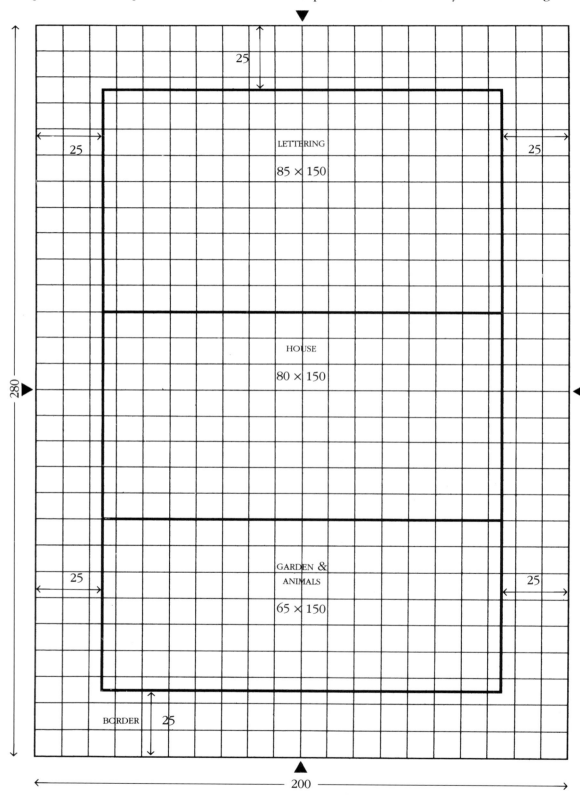

DRAWING YOUR CHART

Take time to work on your chart – the sampler will take a long time to sew and you will invest a great deal of time in it so do not rush the planning stage. The more care you take now the easier the sewing will seem and there will be less need to unpick. Do not plan it all in one session – leave it and after a while return again. Taking a fresh look will help you to spot any changes that are necessary.

To start, trim off the narrow margin on one of the A3 sheets of graph paper. Join the two pieces together on their longest sides. Stick them on the reverse with adhesive tape. This will give you a sheet of graph paper 200 squares wide and 280 squares long on which to work. Use a pencil to mark off a border area 25 squares wide all round. The central area will be 150 squares wide and 230 squares long. Mark the centre of the chart at 100 squares and 140 squares, this will help you when you are arranging your motifs. You can now draw a line dividing this area into three divisions. These lines are just for guidance, if your house is large and your verse quite small they can be changed to suit your requirements.

Start by selecting your main elements: the verse, the house and the type of garden. Draw these elements on separate sheets of graph paper. If you use a motif from a book or magazine, copy just the outline or count the squares and mark this area on separate pieces of graph paper. When you embroider you can work from the original motif but you must mark the space it takes up on your sampler chart beforehand or mistakes will be made.

When you have chosen and charted all the elements for your sampler on separate pieces of graph paper, arrange them on the large sheet, sticking them temporarily with Blu-Tack. Strips of lettering can be cut out and arranged. Centre your lettering by marking the central point on each strip and match it to the centre of the large sheet of graph paper, or make a pleasing arrangement with the central line on the chart acting as a guide. Your border motifs should also be drawn on strips of graph paper, and then stuck on to the plan.

(Opposite) A plan such as this is invaluable at the design stage of your sampler, indicating the position of three distinct areas.

Consider all the elements of your design. If you have a very modern house, a border taken from an eighteenth-century sampler may look peculiar.

When you are satisfied with the arrangement of your motifs and lettering, and feel confident that the proportions are correct and the styles complementary, stick them down with glue. You can now ink over your pencilled lines with your felt-tip pen.

DESIGNING TIPS

If you choose to use ideas from this book but want to add some of your own motifs or lettering, consider the style and size. Will they blend or will the different styles clash? Take trouble when choosing lettering. So many samplers are spoilt by embroiderers concentrating only on the main element, such as their house, and running out of steam when they design their lettering. If you do not have room for the prettiest alphabet – and this always seems to be the case – choose just one capital letter from a favourite alphabet and use it at the beginning of the verse or of each line of the verse.

Remember to keep your main elements in proportion, if your house is large your lettering will look odd if it is too small. You may have to have several attempts at this to get a balance.

It is easy to lose sight of your original idea when you start working on a chart. Make a rough sketch of your planned sampler at the very beginning and keep it by you. This can be fairly basic, and if you are uncomfortable drawing a motif, mark its position with a word instead.

CALCULATING THE SIZE OF YOUR SAMPLER

Now you have drawn your chart, calculate the amount of fabric needed to work your sampler, and the size of the finished piece. To do this divide the number of squares on your chart by the number of threads per inch of your fabric.

WORKING EXAMPLE

Your chart is 200 squares wide by 280 squares long and each square equals one stitch.
The fabrics I have recommended on which to work have 22 and 25 threads per inch.
Allow at least 2 inches on each side for mounting.

This little house is for our friends the
* * * * * * * * * ones we love the best
May each one be a little glad for having
been our guest * * * * * * * * * * *
We cannot all be very rich but we can
* * * * * * * * * * * * * have good cheer
For friendship is our common bond and
we are glad you're here.

Smokey
In the year of
Heidi
1996
Worked by Mary Jenkins

Size of fabric required:

200 × 280 ÷ 22 = 9 × 12.72 + 4 inches = 13 × 16.72 inches

200 × 280 ÷ 25 = 8 × 11.2 + 4 inches = 12 × 15.2 inches

These measurements can now be rounded up. You will need a piece of material on which to practise stitches (see page 27), so make allowance for this now. You only need a piece approximately 4in wide by 10in long.

EQUIPMENT FOR SEWING

Canvas 22 threads per inch
Linen 25 threads per inch
Spare piece of canvas for practising stitches
Frames
Embroidery threads
Small, sharply pointed scissors
Packets of size 22, 24 and 26 tapestry needles
Thread ripper
Thimble
Needle organizer or pincushion
Magnifying glass (optional)

FABRICS

The recommended fabrics used for the projects in this book are canvas with 22 threads per inch and linen with 25 threads per inch. These are the most suitable for this style of work and they have been tried and tested by me over many years. You could work the projects on canvas with 18 threads per inch but you would have to use more thread in your needle and experiment with various thicknesses, and the finished sampler would be much larger.

Linen is available in a great variety of shades and widths but is expensive. Because of this it can be difficult to find a wide variety stocked in non-specialist shops. However, most specialist embroidery shops carry a range and many sell pre-cut sampler-sized pieces. They will advise you if you have difficulty choosing and many will supply by mail and send you small snippets for inspection.

ROSE LODGE
This was worked from the basic sampler plan, though part of the area designated for the border has been used for the rose trees and the name.

ROUGH SKETCH
This is a very rough sketch of my Rose Lodge sampler. I find a sketch such as this essential as it represents the initial idea, which is usually the best!

Linen is the 'Rolls Royce' of fabric and cannot be bettered. It wears well and can be washed if accidents occur; it is not easily crushed in a frame and springs back into shape easily; the needle moves cleanly through it and does not stick. It is worth its price. If you want to work an heirloom that should last 200 years, then this is your fabric!

Canvas, however, is cheaper to buy than linen and though it is made of cotton it should not be washed as it will lose its stiffness. The meshes are more uniform than those of linen and can be seen clearly. This is a great advantage for a beginner. The variety of shades available in canvas is more limited, usually white, off-white and yellow, though 18 threads-per-inch canvas is also available in dark ecru. Most canvas comes in 24-inch widths.

Very many old samplers were worked on linen and that is why they are still around today. In fact many were stitched on very fine linen, far finer than

EQUIPMENT FOR SEWING
A selection of items needed for the working of the
samplers in this book.

is available now. Most of today's embroiderers assume that they cannot work on fine linen and canvas, but it is certainly worth trying as the results are superior to those obtained when working on larger meshed fabrics. Most of us can actually work on a smaller scale mesh than we think we can – eyes really do get tuned in, if they are given time to get accustomed. Maybe all you need is a magnifying glass that can be worn around the neck.

FRAMES

Choosing the embroidery frame that suits your style of working is worth taking time over. It is important to find one that you are comfortable with as wrestling with an unsuitable frame could put you off embroidery. Do not be tempted to work without one as a suitable frame aids working, greatly improves the finished product and cuts down on the time it takes to prepare your work for mounting.

When working with linen I find that wooden ring frames are best. These are cheap and can be bought almost anywhere. Sometimes they can be found in jumble sales. Use a variety of sizes to suit the areas on which you are working. The large area in the middle of your sampler, containing the house and garden, can be worked in a large ring; then move to a medium-sized ring for the lettering; and work around the border on a small ring. Working in this way prevents the embroidery from getting crushed by the frame. To stop the loose material from flapping about and getting soiled, roll it up (not too tightly) and pin it to the side of the frame. Remember to bind your frames and, to keep the binding clean, wash it regularly. I use a narrow finger bandage to bind my frame.

The work must be kept taut to take full advantage of the frame so tighten the screws well. Though linen is a resilient fabric and does not crease easily, it is still better to remove the sampler from the frame between sewing sessions.

Canvas, unlike linen, should not be worked on in a ring frame. For canvas, I use a plastic frame with clips on all four sides. These can be bought in many embroidery outlets, and also direct from the manufacturer. They come in sets, each pack containing lengths of lightweight plastic piping with clips, which can be slotted together to create frames of varying size. Their advantage over the more traditional wooden frames is that they are extremely light and can be quickly and easily dismantled and stored. You can leave your work on this type of frame between sewing sessions – just slacken the pressure by twisting the clips. However, if you want to stop a long-term project in order to work on another, it is easy to adapt this frame for temporary work as no time-consuming processes such as re-stringing are needed. This type of frame will keep the work taut, but if the canvas does slacken as it settles then restore the tension by slipping a piece of material or paper towelling between the clip and the frame.

NEEDLES

Only tapestry needles, which are blunt with a large eye, should be used for the projects in this book. Buy several packets of the same size for if you follow my method you will need many needles. Do not buy packets of assorted sizes – you will probably not use them all. It is very easy to get needle numbers confused so always return them to their original pack between projects. For 22 canvas you will need to use No. 24 tapestry needles, and for 25 linen you will need No. 26 tapestry needles (18 canvas would require No. 22 tapestry needles).

OTHER EQUIPMENT

You will require a good quality pair of small scissors, with a sharp point; a thimble; and a thread ripper with a fine, sharp cutter. Also I use a pincushion as a thread organizer as I work with lots of different needles. I can load them up and park them in the pincushion ready for use.

THREADS

The projects in this book are worked with stranded embroidery cottons (floss), consisting of six strands that can be separated. To achieve a smooth, even stitch, cut a length, separate the six strands and reunite them taking care that the grain of each is running the same way. This process is called 'stripping' the thread and is well worth doing.

All thread ranges have wonderful colour runs and different brands have slightly different tones, this gives a wide variety from which to choose. When I buy a specific thread I usually buy the number preceding and following it as well. If the three threads are used instead of one, the colouring is more subtle and the work richer. It may seem extravagant to work this way but I have found that we all have a favourite palette of colours that we return to constantly and the chances are that we would eventually buy all three shades anyway.

I do not believe in being too tidy. Absolute tidiness inhibits creativity. Of course you need some system, but boxes of perfectly arranged and numbered threads – a separate box for each brand – are unnecessary. I store my threads in clear plastic bags, one for each colour family, mixing all makes. I also have a large bundle of odds and ends of thread ready to dip into when creativity is flowing, especially when working on flowers and plants which only need small amounts of thread.

When planning a flower border you need a balance of colour throughout, just as you would when designing a real garden. Embroidering one is much easier because the plants spring up immediately and you control the colour. For flowers, you need lengths of different shades of one colour. It is a good idea to collect strands of thread from your bundle of odds and ends and display a range of shades for flowers together in a small plastic bag. This 'flower bag' will help you to choose just the right shade when you are sewing – it looks like a

little plot of flowers and will help you to interpret the flower when you are stitching.

Both Anchor and DMC have a range of variegated threads which can be useful for creating shaded effects. Lettering can be made more interesting when shaded and leaves and grass are less flat in variegated green, and the sky has more depth and movement in variegated blue. When using these, do not use the whole skein. Cut it into lengths, light to medium and medium to dark. If you want to save money, and only need small amounts of thread, one variegated skein cut into shaded sections can take the place of several full-sized skeins. Some small manufacturers now produce space-dyed threads which can be found at specialist embroidery shops, needlecraft fairs and through mail order. They are worth seeking out as they come in mouth-watering combinations of colour – almost too beautiful to use. They make lovely borders with different colour combinations emerging as you stitch (see June's Motto on page 113). The results cannot be planned, it all depends on the way the threads have been dyed and the results can be surprising.

The greens in both variegated and space-dyed threads are particularly useful. Use them to form the base of a shrub or creeper and watch the different shades emerging to create realistic results. (See Honeysuckle Cottage page 2 and the leaves on Sampler for June on page 91.)

CHOOSING YOUR COLOURS

When starting a project, choose a colour palette of threads from your collection. To begin with, keep it limited to about twelve colours, bearing in mind that you need light, medium and dark shades to create a pleasing and balanced piece of work.

You must consider the colours you actually need for your motifs and how they will show up against the ground material. If for example you have a pale cream house, it will not stand out if worked on cream linen or canvas. Perhaps you need a stronger cream, or to work it on a darker material. If your cream house has a red roof, your dog is brown and

CORNISH COTTAGE (Opposite)
The slates on the roof and the walls of this Cornish cottage give scope for using all these different shades of greys.

There are eleven shades of grey and blue in the roof and walls of this cottage, worked in differing scales of horizontal cashmere stitch, but quite good results can be obtained with just six shades.

your cat black, these colours are needed in your basic palette of threads. You can then add tones of these colours and some accent colours which will give the work some zip.

A colour should not be too concentrated in any one place but should be distributed throughout the whole of your work. The red of your roof should be used all through your sampler not just isolated to the house in the middle. Use it again in the lettering section, in the garden and on the border.

Here are a few rules, some fairly obvious but worth repeating:

1 Keep all the threads selected for your project in a separate container. You may not use all of them, but they are ready for use and will provide the right balance of colours in light, medium and dark tones.

2 You should have the bundle of thread odds and ends with you when you work and where possible work from this and save your whole skeins. Be frugal where you can!

3 Make a 'flower bag' to keep with your threads.

MIXING AND BLENDING

The way to achieve the effects of subtle colouring – especially in building materials such as stone, brickwork and slate – needs some explanation.

Because I usually work on 22 count canvas using tent stitch over one thread, I have three strands of embroidery cotton (floss) in the needle. Other stitches require more and you will find information regarding this in the thread guide for each stitch. You can mix three threads of adjacent numbers and so achieve many different shades and tones of that colour. It is worth experimenting on your spare piece of canvas.

If the shades are very close in tone some combinations are too subtle and can be lost, especially when working on a small scale. But this method of blending can be adapted to extend your existing thread collection. Experiment with the mix of threads to achieve the effects you want.

You can get good results without mixing when you use closely related groups of coloured threads. To help you to select the colours required for a certain feature, look through magazines and books for a picture or photograph that illustrates the effect you want to achieve and use this as a guide when choosing threads. There may be some shades in the picture that you would not have considered. Match your threads to these colours. Carry the picture with you when buying and selecting threads. Remember, this is where you have an advantage over kit designers. For them economic considerations dictate the number of threads they use and who supplies them, but you are free to select whatever colour and brand you wish.

EMBROIDERERS' GUILD SAMPLER (Opposite)
This sampler was specially designed for the book Making Samplers *and is based on an old sampler in the collection of the Embroiderers' Guild at Hampton Court Palace. It includes many of the stitches featured in this book.*

WELSH COTTAGE
Truda Theodore based her design on a ceramic model of a Breconshire cottage and set it in the landscape of that area which she knows well. The slate roof contains very many shades of blue and grey and is worked in horizontal cashmere stitch, as are the walls, though here they are stitched in differing directions to represent stone.

PREPARING TO SEW

Before working the stitches in all the different shades and combinations of colour, you need to do some preparation and for this you require a number of needles – one for each shade chosen. Load a needle with each colour – if you are working across a roof you may need several sets of colours and needles: work one or two bricks or slates in the first colour (using the appropriate stitch suggested in Chapter Three) and then bring your needle through to the front of the work and rest it there. Then use another colour and then another, always leaving your needle at the front of the work to prevent the threads tangling.

Don't worry too much about the back of the work, you will be working on a limited area at any one time so it won't get too untidy. Keep the picture that inspired you by your side and study it to see how the colours are grouped. Gradually you will see the brickwork emerging in lovely subtle shades – it is very exciting!

You can experiment in this way with many areas of your sampler. If you want to make a hedge look textured, try using the above technique with several greens, using upright cross stitch or diagonal mosaic. The same stitches can be used for a path but this time with terracotta shades (see Weatherboarded Cottage page 54).

The thread combination for working topiary in French knots is quite different. If three close shades were used when working the knot, the subtle differences just wouldn't be visible, so instead you need to combine a light, medium and dark green –

Four shades of terracotta are worked here to depict a brick wall. Note that each shade has its own needle which is kept on the surface of the canvas when not in use.

these greens will emerge in different ways as the threads twist in the needle to form the knot and the resulting embroidered topiary will be rich in both colour and texture.

Remember that all these effects can be practised on a spare piece of canvas. Have a go – it is well worth trying!

DAISY COTTAGE (Opposite)
This little cottage is a dream of mine but its components of brick and thatch are found on cottages in several counties of southern England. This type of border, consisting of different single flowers, is very flexible as the flowers can be arranged with enough space between them to surround any given area.

CHAPTER THREE

The Potential of Stitchery

SINCE Victorian times the most popular stitch for samplers and other types of counted thread embroidery has been cross stitch. It certainly has a good pedigree – it is hardwearing, easy to do and best of all it can be worked in the hand without a frame and the fabric retains its shape. However, having found the 'perfect' stitch we should not simply reject all others, for by working with one stitch only we are ignoring our stitching heritage.

When samplers were first sewn they were used as working tools to record stitches and patterns, and it is thought that some contained as many as forty different stitches. This is difficult to prove even by studying very old samplers as the knowledge of how they were worked has been lost. Many stitches, however, are still with us and by using them we can make our embroideries more beautiful, more interesting to stitch and quicker to complete. I want to encourage you to use these stitches imaginatively, either when working your own design or when working one of the charts in the book. To help you there is a thread guide with every stitch featured, giving thickness of thread and other information.

There are two main groups of stitches, those that cross the intersection of the ground material, for example tent and cross stitch; and those that lie side by side over the threads, such as satin and brick stitch. These groups of stitches do not cover the canvas in the same way. Because they lie on the surface of the canvas, in order to cover it, straight stitches require thicker thread in the needle and it

is sometimes necessary to practise on a spare piece of canvas until you are satisfied with the coverage.

I use tent stitch worked over one thread intersection of the canvas, as my basic stitch. This is quicker and simpler than cross stitch and it combines well with the other stitches. Apart from back stitch it is the smallest stitch, ideal for outlining parts of a design, shading and filling in around other stitches. Outlining the shape in tent stitch first is important, otherwise it would be difficult to know where to begin to plan the layout of the various stitches.

On the following pages you will find details of the stitches I use regularly. Where a stitch is known by more than one name, the alternative(s) are given in brackets. You can learn how to use them by following the numbered diagrams, but they can also be worked more freely to suggest all manner of things.

I choose a stitch to suggest a texture or effect, not just for the sake of using a different stitch – each one should serve a specific purpose. They must give a clear impression and must not look overworked. Remember this simple rule when you are choosing your stitches: for the foreground, larger, more textured stitches can be used, the middle ground should have medium stitches, and the background small-scale smoother stitches.

My stitch sampler, containing one hundred stitches and their variations, is shown opposite. When you reach the end of this chapter, you could work a similar grid for practise using the key on page 49.

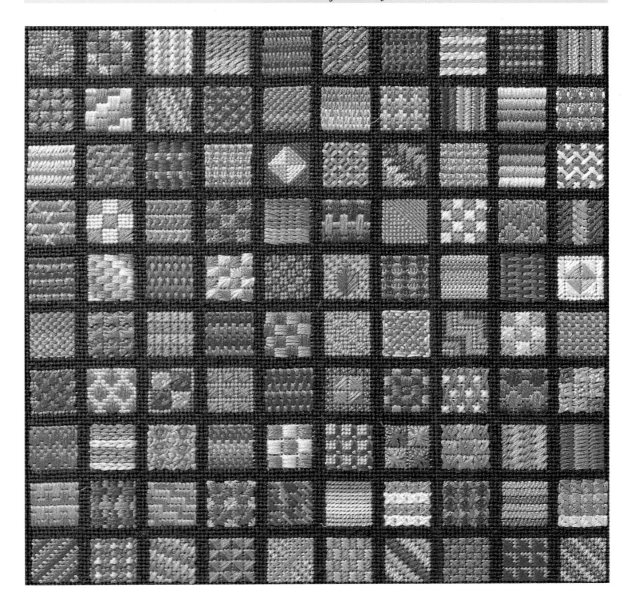

This stitch sampler contains one hundred variations
of the stitches described in this chapter, and took a
long time to work. If you would like to practise the
stitches illustrated in the following pages, you could
work them in a grid to make a smaller version of my
sampler. A suggested grid is given on page 49. This
would help you to get to know the stitches before
using them in a project.

DIAGONALLY WORKED STITCHES

All the stitches in this group are combinations of two basic stitches – tent and slanting gobelin. They are worked over each thread intersection of the canvas producing a smooth and uniform coverage. All can be worked diagonally and horizontally, making this a versatile group of stitches for achieving a wide variety of effects.

TENT STITCH   Continental and Basketweave

THREAD GUIDE   On 22 canvas, 3 threads in a 24 needle

As this is our basic stitch it is important to practise it in all its forms. Make using them second nature so that you can switch from one to another as circumstances demand.

Worked horizontally, tent stitch is called continental stitch and comprises horizontal strokes on the front and long slanting stitches covering the canvas on the reverse side. It is similar to half cross stitch. However, this really is a different stitch as

although it looks the same on the right side it does not cover the back in the same way. Tent stitch is firmer, smoother and wears better than half cross stitch and while durability is not always important in decorative work, I still prefer to use tent stitch. Its main disadvantage, however, is that when it is worked without a frame it can distort the canvas. So in this case you should switch to diagonal tent stitch (sometimes called basketweave). This stitch looks the same as continental stitch on the right side but on the reverse gives a basketweave effect, hence its alternative name. It has the great advantage of not distorting the canvas while you are working.

When following a chart it is extremely difficult to work diagonally so I recommend that you first outline the area to be worked using continental tent stitch and then fill in with diagonal tent stitch. Outlining in tent stitch is important. All stitched areas should be first outlined, then filled in and *covered over* by a larger or more elaborate stitch.

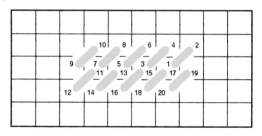

Continental tent stitch

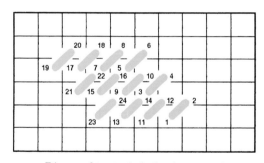

Diagonal tent stitch (basketweave)

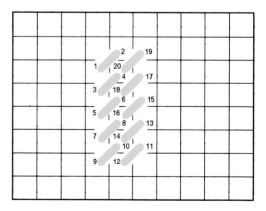

Continental tent stitch worked vertically

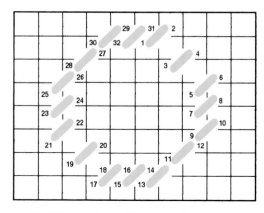

Continental tent stitch outlining an area

Tent stitch can also be worked over alternate threads if a lighter effect is required.

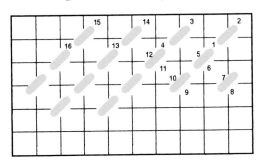

Diagonal skipped tent stitch

SONG OF SOLOMON
Because this was worked on linen with 25 threads per inch I used only a few textured stitches. They would not have shown up working on a small scale except for covering a fairly large area - in this case the Cypress trees.

MOSAIC STITCH   Diagonal and Straight

THREAD GUIDE   On 22 canvas, 3 threads in a 24 needle

This most useful and versatile stitch is a real standby and I use it for many kinds of effects. Because mosaic stitch is a combination of tent stitch and slanting gobelin, it co-ordinates beautifully with tent stitch and the change from one to the other is smooth and subtle.

In its diagonal form, mosaic stitch can be worked densely to represent topiary, hedging and shrubs, or it can be worked randomly with gaps left here and there for a lighter look, simulating free-flowing plants, trees, flowers, foliage and creepers. As its name indicates, it is worked in diagonal rows over one and two threads – try to keep an even tension and do not pull too tightly as this stitch can distort the canvas.

If you decide to fill a large area with this variation of the stitch, first outline the shape in tent stitch and work one line diagonally across the widest part. This will establish the correct angle and flow and you can work the other lines of stitches on both sides of the first line. Any awkward corners can be filled with compensating tent stitches.

The straight form of mosaic stitch gives a more formal look and is best used for architectural rather than for garden effects.

CASHMERE STITCH Diagonal and Horizontal

THREAD GUIDE   On 22 canvas, 3 threads in a 24 needle

Cashmere stitch in its diagonal form is similar to diagonal mosaic stitch, as it, too, is a combination of diagonal stitches on two scales. This enables it to combine easily with tent stitch. However, as it runs across the canvas at a much steeper angle, the similarity between it and diagonal mosaic stitch can be confusing at first, making it more difficult to master. As the difference in angle and construction

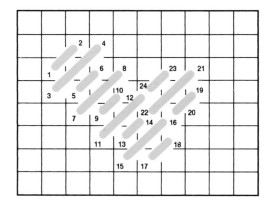

Mosaic stitch, diagonal

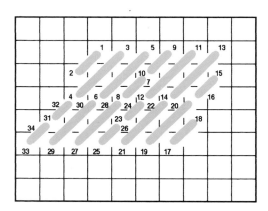

Cashmere stitch, diagonal

Mosaic stitch, straight

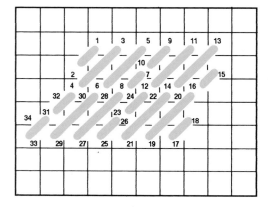

Cashmere stitch, horizontal

gives it a more formal look, it cannot be used freely or randomly for foliage and plants, although it is useful for dense hedging or topiary.

I suggest that you begin by outlining the area you wish to fill with tent stitch and work a line of diagonal cashmere stitch across its widest part. Once you have mastered the angle and rhythm of one line of stitching, the other lines are easier to work and seem to come naturally. Fiddly corner areas and ends of lines can be filled with compensating tent stitches.

Although cashmere stitch worked horizontally is a less well known form, it is very useful for the type of embroidery worked in this book. It can be used on different scales and is well worth learning and practising. I find it invaluable and use it constantly – it appears over and over again in my work. It can be used to represent bricks, slates on roofs and walls, stone work and paving. In a foreground area it can be framed with tent stitch to suggest the pointing between bricks.

CUSHION STITCH   (Scotch stitch)

THREAD GUIDE   On 22 canvas, 3 threads in a 24 needle

Cushion stitch was at one time the general name for the background stitches on canvas, so called because it was first introduced in the embroidering of church kneelers. As with most named stitches, it is actually a grouping of stitches, in this case tent stitch and larger diagonal stitches.

The usefulness of cushion stitch in representing architectural features is limited because it is square – horizontal cashmere with its rectangular shape and similar construction has many more uses for this purpose. However, it is ideal for window panes and can be worked in various directions when the play of light on the threads gives an added dimension (see the Old Post Office on page 66).

For borders, cushion stitch is second to none. It is quickly worked and adaptable, as it can be stitched over an even or uneven number of threads. However, it does distort the canvas, so try to keep a smooth and even tension.

For a beautiful, easy-to-work border, try using space-dyed threads as I have done on the embroidery on this page. A variety of colours will emerge and disappear in an exciting way. It really is cheating, as all the colour selection has been done for you in the dyeing process. Cushion stitch is

This small embroidery features a number of different stitches. The roof is worked in diagonal cashmere in two directions. The windows are worked in framed cushion and cashmere. The base of the house and the walls in the foreground are in cushion and horizontal cashmere. The wall in the middle of the embroidery has been worked in mosaic straight. The sky, patio, hedge, arch, flowers and topiaries are in mosaic diagonal worked in both directions. The border area has been worked in cushion and horizontal cashmere combined with slanting gobelin, using space-dyed threads. I have used variegated threads for the sky, patio and flowers and a single colour space-dyed thread for the arch.

therefore the ideal way to show them to their best advantage.

If this stitch is framed it has quite a different look

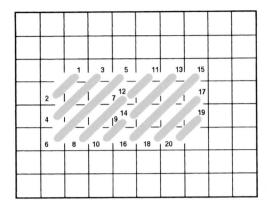

Cushion stitch

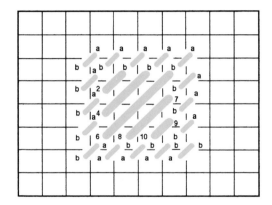

Cushion stitch, framed with tent stitch

as you can see on the wall on the Woodland Crescent sampler on page 99. This variation gives it more detail, making it useful for foregrounds, suggesting differing scales, and as a border stitch.

SLANTING GOBELIN

THREAD GUIDE   On 22 canvas, 3 threads in a 24 needle

I find this stitch most useful and it is probably my favourite stitch of all. It is a larger version of tent stitch and because of this has the same coverage as it lies diagonally across the mesh of the canvas, unlike the other gobelins. It can be worked over a different number of threads to vary its scale, and is quick and effective to work giving instant lustre and richness. I have used it for the weather-boarding on the Kent cottage on page 54, showing how effective it can be.

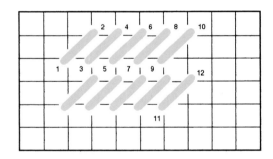

Slanting gobelin

CROSS STITCHES

Made up of two stitches across intersections of canvas, cross stitches are more dense than tent stitches and do not require as many strands of thread in the needle. The quantity of strands sometimes varies, depending on the complexity of the stitch. Therefore, it is always worth having a spare piece of canvas on which to try out stitches with a variety of thicknesses of thread.

CROSS STITCH

THREAD GUIDE   On 22 canvas, 2 threads in a 24 needle

During the nineteenth century this became the favourite stitch for samplers. It is an easy stitch to

master, and is also hardwearing. It can be worked in two ways:

1 Each stitch is completed before moving on to work the next.

2 Work a row of half crosses and then return completing the cross. I call this the 'going and coming' method.

You should choose the one that best suits your purpose. For example, working a block of cross stitches in a dark colour can be hard on the eyes and you may find it easier to complete the cross before moving to the next stitch. However, if you are working lettering, it is easier to form the letter by stitching half of each cross, completing them on the return journey and ending back where you started.

Cross stitch is the best stitch to use for larger lettering. It makes a perfectly formed letter and in this instance, is superior to tent stitch which can make letters appear unbalanced.

When working a block of cross stitches, the main rule to remember is that while it does not matter which way you cross the stitches, you must be consistent or the texture will be uneven.

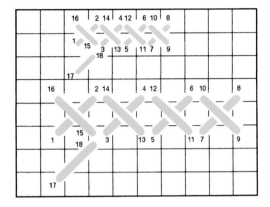

Cross stitch, worked over one thread (top) and two threads (below)

If you find two threads too thick when working the 'going and coming' method, use two threads one way and return with one thread. This trick can also be used to tone down a colour, using darker thread one way and a lighter one on the return.

DOUBLE CROSS AND SMYRNA CROSS STITCH

THREAD COUNT On 22 canvas, 2 threads in a 24 needle

Worked singly these stitches can look like flowers, blocks of them can depict trees, bushes or standards in plant pots.

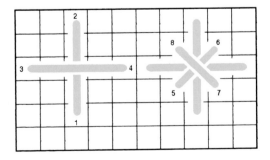

Double cross stitch

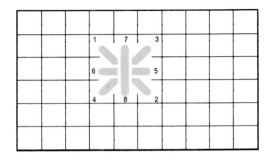

Smyrna cross stitch

OBLONG CROSS STITCH

THREAD GUIDE On 22 canvas, 2 threads in a 24 needle

This looks different to a traditional cross stitch but the method of working is the same as the more common version. Oblong cross stitch can be used to work a tree but can also decorate the ridge of a thatched roof or even depict a trellis porch.

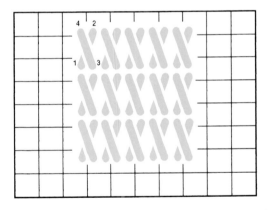

Oblong cross stitch across one and up two threads

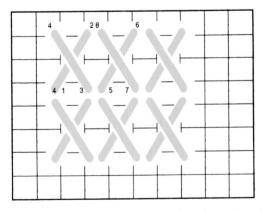

Oblong cross stitch across two and up three threads

VELVET STITCH

THREAD COUNT On 22 canvas, 2 threads in a 24 needle

Velvet stitch is a cross stitch with a loop in the middle and was used widely in Victorian canvaswork. Unlike most other stitches, it should be worked from bottom to top so that the loops do not get in the way when you add the next row. Do not take your thumb off the loop until the cross is completed or it will come apart. After working, the loops can be cut for a 'velvety' look or they can be left uncut, providing most realistic bushes.

I usually work the uncut version of this stitch. You will see it as a tree in Dorset Dream on page 40, worked with two shades of green thread, and as standards in tubs opposite worked with space-dyed green threads to add interesting colour tones.

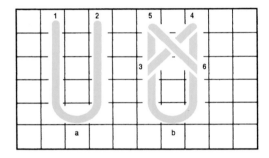

Velvet stitch

This sampler was designed to show the potential of using cross stitches together with Norwich and velvet stitch which are part of the cross stitch family. There are also some areas in tent and slanting gobelin stitch for a change of texture. The clipped trees worked in uncut velvet stitch with their tubs in large-scale Norwich stitch surrounded by cross stitch.

The outer border is worked in Norwich stitch on two scales, in multicoloured space-dyed threads combined with slanting gobelin in the same thread and some cross stitch worked over four threads of the canvas. The inner border is rice stitch and the trellis area oblong cross stitch – working like this is an extremely quick way to fill up large areas of canvas. The inner area of foliage surrounding the cottage is worked in cross, upright cross, oblong cross and double cross stitches, and the tubs of flowers in cross, smyrna cross, upright cross and double cross stitches, with some French knots. The central trellis area consists of a block of green tent stitches overlaid with cross stitch worked over four threads.

RICE STITCH (William and Mary)

THREAD COUNT   On 22 canvas, 2 threads in a 24 needle

This is a very old stitch found on early spot samplers. It is rather large and formal to use within the main body of a picture but it makes a very good decorative border.

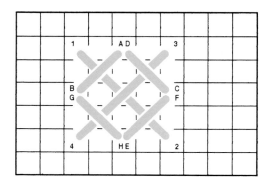

Rice stitch

NORWICH STITCH   (Waffle stitch)

THREAD GUIDE   On 22 canvas, 2 threads in a 24 needle

This stitch is large and spectacular, especially good for working on the border area of your picture. You can see Norwich stitch worked in space-dyed threads in the top corners and bottom border area of the embroidery on pages 36 and 37, and the Versailles tubs were created by framing the large-scale version of the stitch with cross stitches.

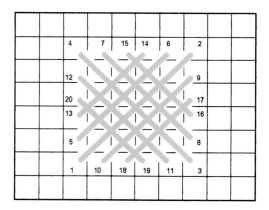

Norwich stitch over five threads

The large-scale version of Norwich stitch (over 12 threads) uses a long length of thread because it is not easy to join in new thread whilst in the middle of working this quite complicated stitch. So make sure that you have enough thread in the needle to complete each stitch.

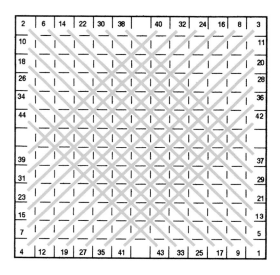

Norwich stitch over twelve threads

UPRIGHT CROSS STITCH

THREAD GUIDE   On 22 canvas, 2 threads in a 24 needle

This is my favourite cross stitch. It is small, neat and versatile and can be worked straight or diagonally. Worked in one colour it makes an excellent tiled roof but by working with different shades in separate needles more natural effects can be achieved for shrubs and hedges. It can also be worked randomly to represent flowers.

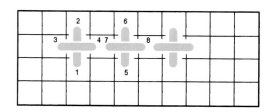

Upright cross stitch

STRAIGHT STITCHES

The next group of stitches are worked by laying the stitches side by side on the surface of the canvas and they usually need a thicker thread in the needle than the cross stitches. This stitch group includes the extremely useful gobelin stitches. Gobelin is the traditional name for satin or straight stitch. Because early canvaswork was intended to imitate the much admired and very expensive woven tapestries it is understandable that its basic stitch was named after the famous Gobelin tapestry factory. This is also why canvas embroidery or needlepoint is known, incorrectly, as tapestry work.

STRAIGHT GOBELIN   (Satin stitch)

THREAD GUIDE   On 22 canvas, 5 threads in a 24 needle

This is the basic stitch usually worked over two or three threads. When worked conventionally in rows, it has a ridged appearance which limits its usefulness, though it makes excellent steps. It is very simple to work but must be smooth and even, so it is most important that you strip your threads (see page 21) before working this stitch.

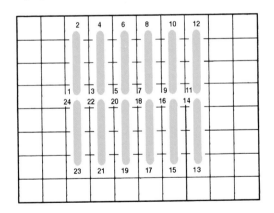

Straight gobelin

OBLIQUE GOBELIN

THREAD GUIDE   On 22 canvas, 3 threads in a 24 needle

This is a slightly slanting version of the gobelin stitch and, like straight gobelin, when worked in rows is also ridged. It can be worked vertically which makes it a good edging stitch. I use this version for window sills, window surrounds and roof ridges.

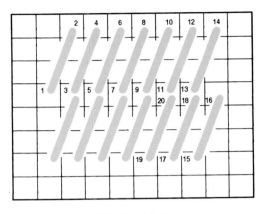

Gobelin oblique

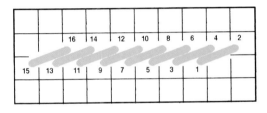

Gobelin oblique worked vertically

ENCROACHING GOBELIN   (Interlocking)

THREAD GUIDE   On 22 canvas, 3 threads in a 24 needle

This stitch can be straight or slanted and, as it has a smoother and less ridged appearance than some of the other gobelin stitches, it is wonderful for conveying shading. It can be worked either vertically and horizontally to represent sky, or vertically only to represent thatch.

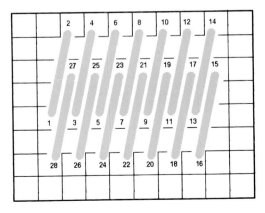

Encroaching gobelin

DORSET DREAM
*This small Dorset cottage has a thatched roof worked
in split gobelin, chimneys in straight gobelin, and a
path and window sills in oblique gobelin.*

SPLIT GOBELIN

THREAD GUIDE   On 22 canvas, 2 threads in a 24 needle

Similar to encroaching gobelin, all the same uses can be applied to split gobelin. This stitch is extremely smooth. It makes an excellent thatch.

Only two threads are required in the needle when working this stitch, as every row is split into by the row below. However, as the final row is not split it is necessary to use a thicker thread (three threads in the needle) for coverage.

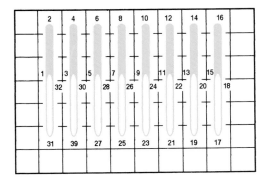

Split gobelin

FLORENTINE   (Bargello, Hungarian point, Flame and Irish stitch)

THREAD GUIDE   On 22 canvas, 5 threads in a 24 needle

If Florentine is worked correctly the back of the canvas will be covered with stitches as well as the front – this is why it has always been popular for cushions and other items that recieve wear and tear. Even though this coverage is not so important when working a picture to be framed, it is best to learn the stitch correctly as illustrated below.

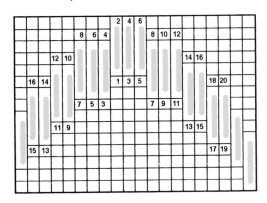

Florentine

Florentine is an arrangement of stitches rather than an actual stitch, the basic stitch being straight gobelin, but when used in various counted combinations creates effects such as pinnacles and curves.

Florentine can be used for dividing bands and borders. By working a single line of stitches we can create the ridge of a thatch roof or the arch of a Gothic window, which is useful as curves in architecture are difficult to show in any other way.

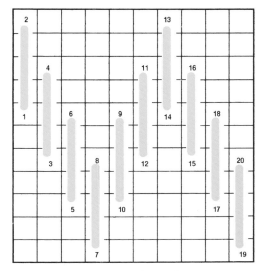

Florentine for peaks

HUNGARIAN STITCH

THREAD GUIDE   On 22 canvas, 5 threads in a 24 needle

This is a grouping of straight gobelins and can be worked on different scales. I use it in its smallest form to represent roofs, paths or diamond pane windows. It can represent stylized shrubs in pots and is also a very practical stitch for borders.

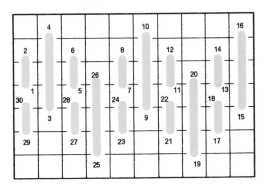

Hungarian stitch

TWILL STITCH

THREAD GUIDE   On 22 canvas, 5 threads in a 24 needle

Twill stitch is worked over *uneven threads* and is worked in a similar way to brick stitch. It has a smoother appearance and can be shaded, making it suitable for the tiled roof in the Kent cottage (see page 55). To achieve the effect of its subtle colouring, load the needle with various shades of the same colour, in this case brown and terracotta.

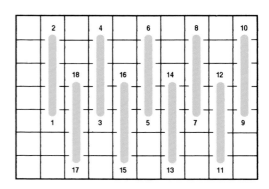

Brick stitch over four threads

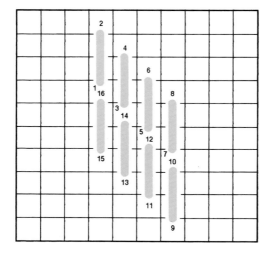

Twill stitch

PATTERN DARNING

THREAD GUIDE   On 22 canvas, 2 threads in a 24 needle

This is the simplest darning stitch to be found among a group of different darning patterns which were sometimes used on old samplers. It can be used over one or two threads and can be worked in groups of two.

I use it as an alternative to brick stitch for small-scale areas of brickwork on chimneys and porches and it is very easy and quick to work.

As space is left between each stitch and each row, only two threads are required in the needle as it is not necessary to cover the canvas.

BRICK STITCH

THREAD GUIDE   On 22 canvas, 5 threads in a 24 needle

This is a straight stitch worked over *even threads –* two and four are the most useful for our purposes. Worked over two horizontal threads it is effective for small-scale brickwork on chimneys and over four vertical threads will make excellent conifers and Cypress trees.

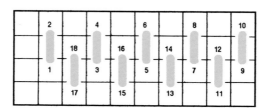

Brick stitch over two threads

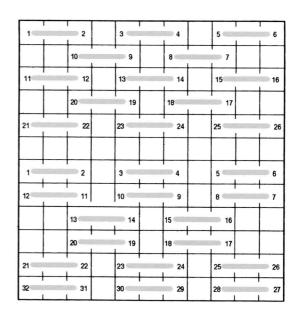

Pattern darning over one and two threads

BACK STITCH

THREAD GUIDE   1 thread in the needle gives a clear outline

This stitch can be used for outlining an area of architecture or to give greater definition to an animal. It is also extremely useful for small-scale lettering, but do make sure that your thread colour choice is dark enough to show up at a distance. For outlining, it is usual to work over one or two threads but to achieve the smooth line required for lettering, fences, outlining door panels, indicating window bars and latticing, lay the stitch over a greater number of threads.

TOLL HOUSE ROOF
This may well appear to be a complicated roof but once its shape is outlined in tent stitch the space to be filled is really quite small. Three shades of blue were used for the slates with straight mosaic stitch for the central part and diagonal mosaic for the sides. The stitch is sloped in different directions to suggest perspective.

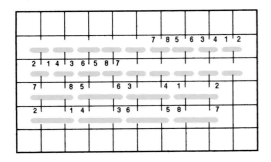

Back stitch worked over one or two threads

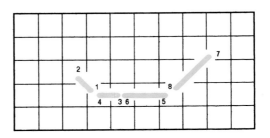

Back stitch outlining worked over one, two or more threads

USEFUL DECORATIVE STITCHES

The following textured stitches are extremely useful for creating many different effects. Experiment with them to find new ways of using them.

LEAF STITCH

THREAD GUIDE   On 22 canvas, 2 threads in a 24 needle for small leaves and 3 threads for large leaves

This can be worked on a variety of scales and angles. They are highly textured and extremely attractive stitches and once mastered are fairly quick to work. They are very effective when worked in variegated and space-dyed threads (see Sampler for June on page 91). They can be used either formally or freely.

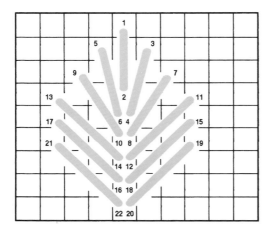

Large leaf stitch

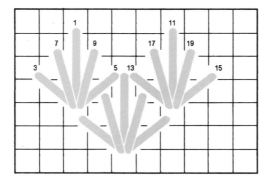

Small leaf stitch

(Opposite)

This embroidery was designed to demonstrate some of the uses of leaf, rococo and eyelets.

The conifer trees show how effective leaf stitch can be when worked over a large area. The stitches in the conifer trees are worked on two scales, the nearest over nine threads and the second over eight. This tiny change, though hardly discernible, aids perspective and the green space-dyed thread creates slight changes of tone. Other variations of leaf stitch are included, a bush is worked in a small-scale stitch and other leaves are randomly worked.

Three variations of rococo stitch are used together with French stitch used for the lupins in the foreground. Diagonal rococo is used for the decorative panes of glass in the door, with the longer version of rococo included depicting flowers as well as the standard version used for shrubs and foliage.

The eyelets in this picture are freely worked to represent all types of leaves and flowers. They are sometimes combined with small and large French knots to resemble daisy-type flowers and the lupin leaves in the foreground are worked in thick space-dyed thread.

The border was worked quickly in slanting gobelin over eight threads of canvas using a multicoloured space-dyed thread which echoes and strengthens the colours within. The smoothness of the slanting gobelin gives a change of texture which, combined with its large scale, shows off the range of colours in the thread.

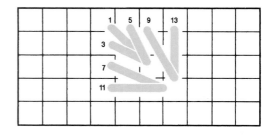

Diagonal leaf stitch

Count no men poor who have
the stars above,
The peace and quietude of
evening hours
And in their hearts that rarest
gift of love
And in their garden-flowers.

FRENCH KNOT

It is difficult to be precise on the number of threads in the needle to work a French knot. It depends on the effects you require and for that you will need to practise the stitch on a spare piece of canvas. I feel it is better to have a small number of strands in the needle and work more loops, for an airier effect.

Although it is not really a canvaswork stitch the French knot is extremely useful for many decorative effects. It can be worked tightly or loosely, small or large, depending on the number of loops on the needle and how tightly they are pulled through the canvas. It is great fun to work and gives tremendous scope for depicting all types of flowers and dense shrubs.

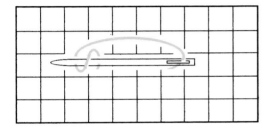

French knot

EYELETS

Use one strand in your needle so you can keep working over the foundation threads until you have achieved the density you want.

Algerian eye is a squared eyelet, and was an extremely popular stitch on old samplers. It was used for alphabets, flowers, borders and dividing bands. Eyelets can be round, diamond-shaped or freely worked, but all must be worked from the outside to a central hole and the thread pulled firmly to keep the stitch smooth, but not too tight or it will pull the canvas out of shape.

JANET'S GARDEN
This embroidery by Janet Davies is a tour de force in French knots. Both the topiary and the standard trees framing the sundial are worked in this stitch demonstrating how effective it can be. The flowers in the foreground are worked in space-dyed threads and slanting and straight gobelin stitches are used for the steps and path. The sundial is worked in very long laid threads.

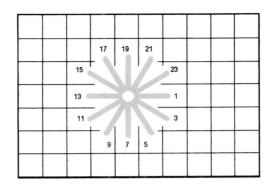

Round eyelet

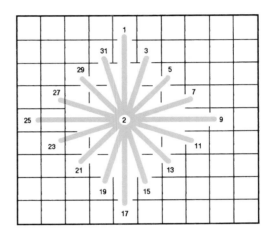

Diamond eyelet

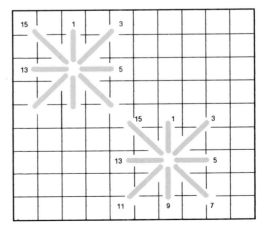

Square eyelet

ROCOCO STITCH (Queen stitch)

THREAD GUIDE   On 22 canvas, 1 thread in a 24 needle

This stitch was widely used on seventeenth-century samplers and needlework pictures. It is highly textural and very distinctive. Although it is complicated to work it is well worth mastering and can be used where interesting texture is required. To show the complex texture of this stitch at its best use a fine thread in the needle. I have used it for a basket with sleeping cat (on page 95) and it depicts pargetting on the East Anglian Cottage (page 110). You can use its diagonal form for highly decorative effects like the ones you find on modern concrete wall blocks. It could be used for wrought-iron window bars or gates or panels in railings.

It is challenging to find new uses for this stitch and so preserve it in our stitch vocabulary, not just because it is beautiful and it has been used for hundreds of years, but because it really does work in new settings.

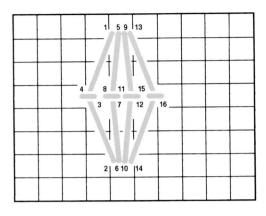

Long rococo stitch

FRENCH STITCH

THREAD GUIDE   On 22 canvas, 1 thread in a 24 needle

This is half of a rococo stitch and can be used for a variety of textural effects.

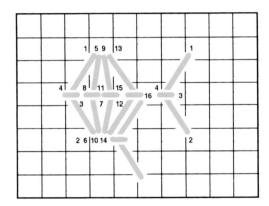

Standard rococo stitch

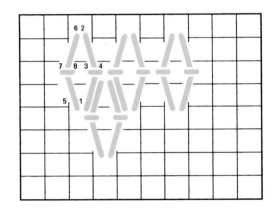

French stitch

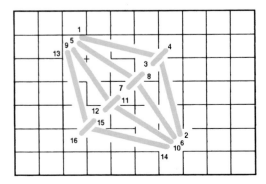

Diagonal rococo stitch

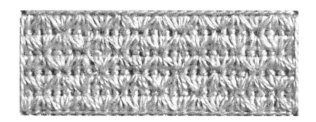

Detail of pargetting taken from the East Anglian cottage (page 110), showing the textured effect of rococo stitch.

MAKE YOUR OWN STITCH SAMPLER

1	2	3	4	5	6
7	8	9	10	11	12
13	14	15	16	17	18
19	20	21	22	23	24
25	26	27	28	29	30
31	32	33	34	35	36

You may wish to make a stitch sampler similar to the one shown on page 29, to practise the stitches in this chapter. Work your sampler on 22 canvas or 18 canvas; form the grid first by working three tent stitches, and leaving 20 meshes of canvas in between.

1 Skipped tent
2 Diagonal cashmere
3 Double cross
4 Upright cross
5 Split gobelin
6 Hungarian
7 Diagonal mosaic
8 Cushion
9 French
10 Straight mosaic
11 Rice
12 Encroaching gobelin
13 Pattern darning single
14 Diamond eyelet
15 Oblique gobelin
16 Square eyelet
17 Straight gobelin
18 Diagonal rococo
19 Pattern darning double
20 Oblong cross single
21 Diagonal leaf
22 Smyrna cross
23 Large leaf
24 Standard rococo
25 Twill
26 Straight cashmere
27 Brick over two threads
28 Long rococo
29 Oblong cross double
30 Round eyelet
31 Gobelin oblique vertically
32 Framed cushion
33 Norwich
34 Brick over four threads
35 Small leaf
36 Slanting gobelin

CHAPTER FOUR

Houses

On the following pages are a selection of embroidered houses together with their charts. Use them to make a sampler or a small picture. Some are featured on larger samplers but most have been specially designed for this book, and worked by me or one of my friends. These charts were drafted from the basic house shape on page 78 and all will fit the basic sampler plan on page 16.

Having read the previous chapter, you should by now understand the potential of all the different stitches explained in it. You can fill the spaces on the charts with a combination of these stitches.

The charts are shown in outline only. This is deliberate as it would be impossible to chart them in a way that could be easily understood. First outline the various parts of the house indicated on the chart in tent stitch. The skeleton of the house will appear on your canvas for you to fill in with your chosen stitches. You need not use the ones I have used; you may like to try others. In that way your house will be personal and not just a copy.

Each chart shows only the house, I have not included any of the flowers, creepers, shrubs or animals that may appear in the accompanying picture. This is also deliberate, I have not cluttered up the chart by trying to depict all the features because you will find it easier to choose and make up your own, or even copy mine from the picture.

Let the colour picture be your guide. It may help if you enlarged both picture and chart by photo-copying them. To give further flexibility, make notes on your copy of the chart or mark off an area you want to cover with a different stitch. Pencil in a porch that you have seen elsewhere in the book, draw in a creeper or add anything else. Sometimes it is easier to change something that has already been drawn than to start from scratch.

Each house photograph is accompanied by a key of the stitches and colour palette I have used.

I hope by now that I have convinced you that using the stitches suggested is not difficult. However all the charts can be worked completely in tent stitch, or why not just try one or two new stitches and work the rest in tent stitch. This will introduce you gradually into the wonderful world of stitchery.

ORDER OF WORKING

1 Work the door and window frames *only*.
2 Outline the roof area in tent stitch with *one* thread in your needle. The outline tent stitches will be covered by your chosen stitch, so choose a shade that will not show through.
3 You can similarly indicate the edges of walls and chimneys in tent stitch.
4 Now you have the framework of your house you can fill it with any chosen stitch knowing that the sizes are correct and the features are in the right place. Following are details of the stitches I prefer to use for particular features, but do experiment with your own stitches.

NOTE: In the previous chapter, I explained that often a stitch has several names or that some stitches, when worked as a group, become known by a different name and this can be very confusing: for example cashmere stitch is simply a worked group of slanting gobelin stitches. I have used both terms in the working description and chart key for each house, but if in doubt about a stitch study the photograph for clarification.

TIPS FOR STITCHING

WINDOWS

Windows give a house its character. If a person's eyes are pale the face does not make an immediate impact – so too with windows; if the colour chosen for them is too light, the facade of the house can look dull and rather uninteresting. While the window frames can be any colour of your choosing, I find that panes look best in dark grey, blue and turquoise. I usually favour white frames and bars which contrast well, but if you decide to use black for the frames and leaded lights, to make sure they stand out sufficiently against the glass panes, choose a slightly lighter

A variation of the Flint Cottage, on page 57, has been worked by Clare Probert. By altering a few of the features and choosing different stitches any of the designs in this chapter can be personalized.

shade of the three recommended colours.

If you are working windows with large panes of glass, take care as large blocks of a dark colour can dominate the whole design. You can make large windows look more interesting and less over-whelming if you suggest curtains by using a lighter shade of thread near the frame. You can use either straight rows of stitching or you can shape them (see the bay window on Louise's House on page 81).

I usually work frames in tent stitch and slanting gobelin and these two stitches plus cashmere are also my favourites for working window panes in general. Many windows have quite elaborately formed bars and leaded lights and you will need to use stitches such as upright cross, diagonal mosaic and Hungarian to create such patterns. Basic window bars, however, are easily formed with a row of tent stitches or by laying long threads, with the sills and surrounds of the windows being stitched in either slanting or oblique gobelin.

DOORS

A door gives great character to a house and its colour can make a difference, not only to the house, but also to the picture as a whole. If the composition is beginning to look rather uniform, choosing a vibrant colour for the door will give it the required fillip.

When choosing stitches, much depends on the door style; I often work it in blocks of cashmere to suggest panels, surrounded by rows of slanting gobelin, working both stitches in different directions.

Detail from the Victorian Lodge (page 64). The shape of this window is achieved by using Florentine stitches to form the curve of its lintel and frame. Threads are overlaid to suggest the lattice bars. The surround and sill are worked in slanting gobelin.

Detail from Kent cottage (page 54). The door is worked in large-scaled cashmere and slanting gobelin blocks, and to show the panels I have worked them in alternate directions. The door surround is worked in slanting gobelin and the steps in straight gobelin.

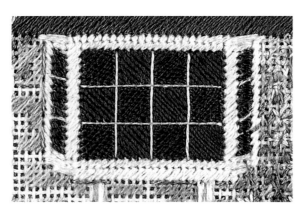

Detail from the Old Post Office (page 66). The shallow sloping lines used to indicate the shape of bay and oriel windows are suggested by laying long threads. I have worked the side windows in oblique gobelin, sloping the stitches in opposite directions to show the slant of the window panes and ending them one row above the middle window to show perspective. The middle panes are worked in cushion stitch in alternate directions to add shadowing.

Detail from Honeysuckle Cottage (page 2). This door has been worked by alternating rows of tent stitch with slanting gobelin. A row of straight gobelin forms the baseboard, with its ends worked in slanting gobelin to add perspective. The porch roof is worked in oblique gobelin and filled with tent stitch, and its details and angles are suggested by laying long threads. The bricks at the base of the porch are created by pattern darning.

ROOFS

Old buildings were generally roofed in slate, stone, clay tiles or thatch, probably quarried or harvested locally so giving an identity and cohesiveness to the area. While this is still true of conservation areas today, economic considerations mean that most modern houses are roofed in mass-produced materials such as concrete tiles, so regional differences are disappearing.

Detail from Rose Lodge (page 18). This is a roof of stone slate based on one seen in Yorkshire. I used a magazine photograph to select the colours, and without this reference source I would not have chosen such a variety of threads as I would not have believed there were so many subtle changes of colour in one roof! I have used cashmere stitch with the various colours in different needles, referring to the photograph to help me to group the colours. The ridge has been worked in straight gobelin and back stitch.

Detail from Old Post Office (page 66). This roof of old clay tiles is typical of those found throughout the south-east of England. The tiles are worked in cashmere stitch using a space-dyed thread of many shades of terracotta. With a space-dyed thread you only need one needle as the variation in the colours is in the thread itself. While this makes working easier, you will have less control over the end result.

CHIMNEYS

There are a great number of chimney styles and they are made in a tremendous variety of materials. But the house is the star of our sampler and the chimney plays only a small part, so we must content ourselves with modest chimneys worked in small-scale stitches or they could overwhelm the house.

I usually work the stacks in either brick stitch or pattern darning and give a change of texture by using either slanting gobelin or cushion stitch for the pots. Chimneys were very often made of a completely different material to that of the roof; but even if they were not, they might well have been painted a different colour, which all makes for a more interesting roof line.

Detail from Rose Lodge (page 18). This chimney is in four parts: the lower stack is worked in pattern darning, and the upper stack, its ridge and the pot itself are all worked in slanting gobelin.

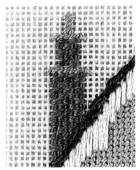

Detail from Victorian Lodge (page 64). This chimney stack is worked in brick stitch, the ridge in oblique gobelin and the pot is a cashmere stitch.

Detail from Stone Manor (page 62). This pair of stone stacks and chimneys are worked in blocks of slanting gobelin with the tops of the stacks indicated by long laid threads.

WEATHER-BOARDED COTTAGE, KENT

This is one of the easiest of the cottages to stitch as its outline is very similar to the basic house shape (see page 78). Although it appears to be made of wood, this is not so. The weather-boarding acts as cladding for the walls, and is put there to give them extra protection from the weather.

Start by working the door and window frames in slanting gobelin stitch. Then outline the roof with tent stitch and fill it with twill stitch. The chimneys can now be worked using pattern darning. Fill each of the windows with blocks of cashmere stitch to represent the panes of glass and make the window bars by laying thread along the divisions formed between the panes. Work the door in blocks of slanting gobelin stitch, and the steps and porch in straight gobelin stitch. Use the picture as your guide while you are stitching.

If you want to add a flower border or a climbing rose, work them *before* covering the walls with weather-boarding using slanting gobelin stitch.

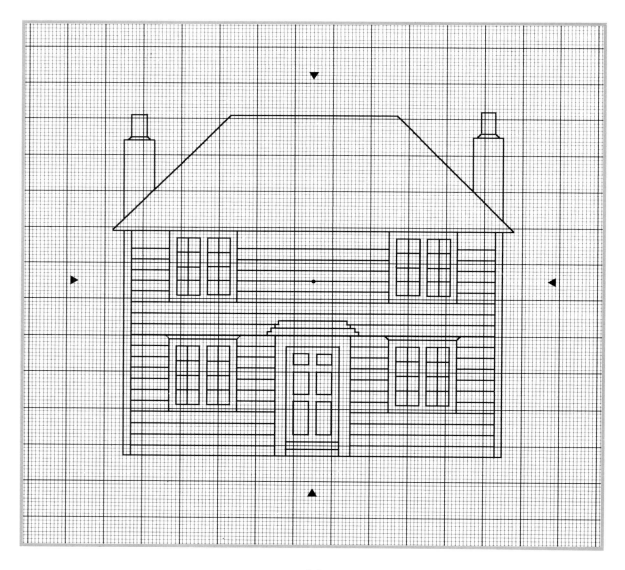

WEATHER-BOARDED COTTAGE, KENT
Key to colours and stitches

CHIMNEYS			WINDOWS		
Pots	Tent	DMC 356	Frames	Slanting gobelin	White
Stacks	Pattern darning	DMC 356	Panes	Cashmere	Anchor 851
Outline	Back	DMC 3022	Bars	Laid threads	White
ROOF			PORCH	Straight gobelin	DMC 3022
Ridge and coping tiles	Oblique gobelin	Anchor 338			
			DOOR	Cashmere and slanting gobelin	DMC 312
Main roof	Twill	Mixture of Anchor 338, 884 and DMC 632	STEPS	Straight gobelin	DMC 642
Guttering	Oblique gobelin	DMC 645	WEATHER-BOARD	Slanting gobelin	White

FLINT COTTAGE

This cottage, worked by Jean Davies, is situated on the border of Hampshire and West Sussex. Flint has always been a popular building material in many parts of southern and eastern England, particularly in river valleys – although similar cottages, also with thatched roofs, can be found many miles further west in Dorset. Brick is used with the flint for shaping around windows and doors. This combination of building materials makes an interesting mix of textures and colours.

Start by working the door in slanting gobelin stitch and the window frames in two rows of tent stitch. Outline the roof (leaving a gap for the chimney area) with tent stitch. Work the chimney in cushion stitch and the brick stack in cashmere.

Next work the roof, using straight gobelin stitch for the ridge and the edge, and using split gobelin stitch for the main area. Deal with the porch roof in the same way. Work the windows with blocks of cashmere stitch to represent the panes and lay threads between the cashmere stitches to represent the window bars. Now work the areas of brick around the windows.

If you want to add climbers and flower borders, now is the time to do so. The pointing between the bricks is worked by overlaying cream thread between the bricks. The flint can now be added using freely worked diagonal mosaic stitch.

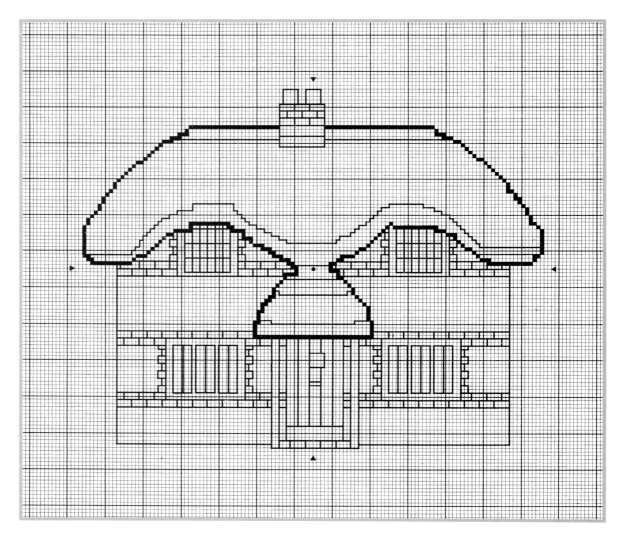

56

FLINT COTTAGE
Key to colours and stitches

CHIMNEY			WALLS		
Pots	Cushion	Anchor 884	Flint	Freely worked diagonal mosaic	Anchor 398, 399, DMC 642
Stack	Cashmere	Anchor 883, 884			
			Bricks	Cashmere	Anchor 883, 884
ROOF					
Ridge and edge	Straight gobelin	DMC 371	Pointing	Laid threads	Anchor 590
Thatch	Split gobelin	DMC 370, 371, Anchor 888	WINDOWS		
			Frames	Tent	White
			Panes	Cashmere	DMC 317
DOOR	Slanting gobelin	DMC 931	Bars	Long overlaid threads	White
PORCH SUPPORT	Slanting gobelin	DMC 370			

CORNISH COTTAGE

The main feature of this little cottage is its slate-clad walls which protect it from the very rough weather which sweeps over Cornwall from the Atlantic. Slate, which has been quarried in the area for hundreds of years, weathers to wonderful subtle shades. This, as you can see in the example worked by Janet Davies, provides scope for using a variety of grey and blue threads.

Start by outlining the roof of the porch and house in tent stitch, then work the frame of the door and walls of the porch in slanting gobelin. The boarding on the porch is created with rows of oblique gobelin and the roof of the porch is stitched with straight gobelin. The upper window frames are worked in tent stitch and oblique gobelin, and the lower frames are worked in slanting gobelin. The window bars are tent stitch and laid threads. The window panes comprise tent stitch, the lower ones stitched in two shades of grey to suggest curtains. Work the chimney stack in tent stitch with an edge of straight gobelin. The roof ridge is also worked in straight gobelin, and the guttering in slanting gobelin. The roof can now be filled with various shades of grey cashmere. The upper wall slates are worked irregularly in blocks of cashmere in a variety of shades. The lower walls are worked in tent stitch and the door step in straight gobelin. The four corners of the porch are decorated with Smyrna cross stitch.

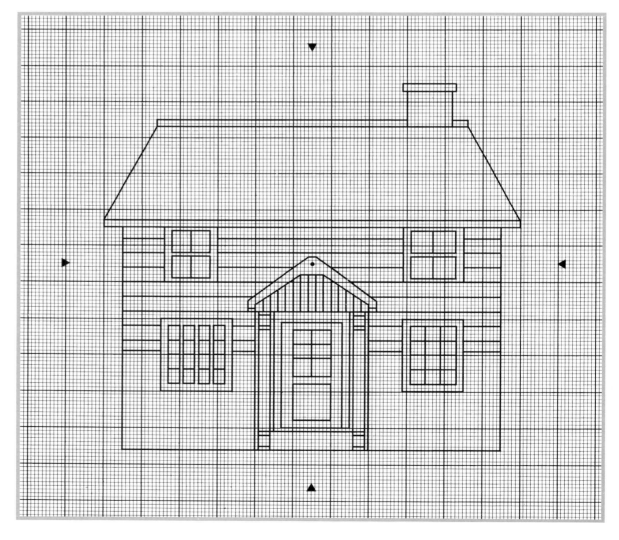

CORNISH COTTAGE
Key to colours and stitches

CHIMNEY			WINDOWS		
Stack	Tent	Anchor 847	Frames	Tent, oblique and slanting gobelin	White
Edges	Straight gobelin	DMC 317			
			Panes	Tent	DMC 844
ROOF			Curtains	Tent	DMC 414
Ridge	Straight gobelin	DMC 317	Bars	Tent and laid threads	White
Main roof	Cashmere	DMC 317, 414, 415, 451			
			PORCH		
			Roof	Straight gobelin	DMC 317
Guttering	Slanting gobelin	DMC 317	Boarding	Oblique gobelin	White
			Sides	Tent and slanting gobelin	DMC 3024
WALLS					
Upper	Cashmere	DMC 926, 927, 928, 3023, 3024, Anchor 847, 920	Decoration	Smyrna cross	DMC 317
			DOOR		
			Main door	Slanting gobelin	Anchor 211
			Outer frame	Slanting gobelin	DMC 451
Lower	Tent	Anchor 847	Step	Straight gobelin	DMC 3024

WELSH BORDER FARMHOUSE

This type of black and white house can be found in the West Midlands of England and the Welsh Borders. Oak has always been plentiful and widely used in the area. It hardened through the centuries to make these half-timbered houses so durable that they still remain for us to enjoy today. This one, worked by Truda Theodore, is roofed with stone slates and has a stone base and brick chimneys. The shape is simple but the colours and textures of the building materials, in particular its lattice windows, depicted in blue and black with yellow frames, make it an attractive house to embroider.

Begin by working the door and outlining the windows, roof and chimneys in tent stitch. Fill the roof with blocks of cashmere and the chimney stacks with brick stitch. Work the chimney in cushion stitch. Fill the upper windows with upright cross stitch and the lower ones in Hungarian stitch. Next the gables can be worked in straight gobelin and the beams in slanting gobelin stitch. The window frames are created by laying long threads between the beams and windows. The porch roof and walls are worked in tent stitch. Next the stone at the base of the house can be worked in large blocks of slanting gobelin. The walls are worked in white tent stitch and their small beams are overlaid in black thread. The area of the walls between the beams can now be filled with large-scale slanting stitches which give a smooth texture and are very quick to work.

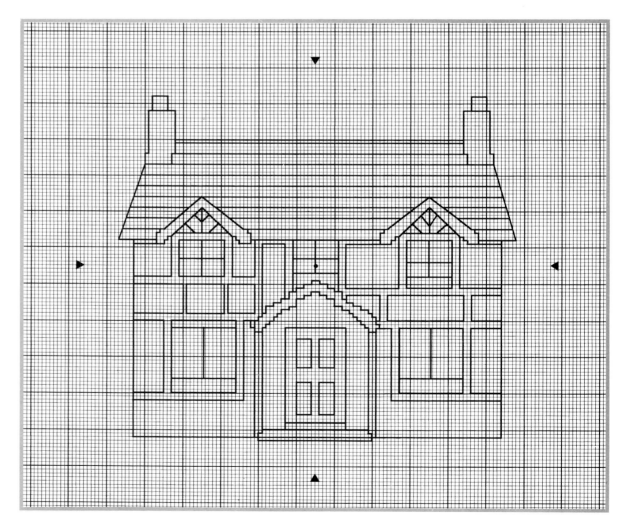

WELSH BORDER FARMHOUSE
Key to colours and stitches

CHIMNEYS		
Pots	Cushion	Anchor 853
Stacks	Brick	DMC 301, 407
Outline	Back	DMC 301

ROOF		
Ridge	Oblique gobelin	DMC 642
Main roof	Cashmere	Anchor 853, DMC 3023, 3024, 3032, 611, 612

GABLES	Straight gobelin	DMC 844

BEAMS	Slanting gobelin and overlaid threads	DMC 844

WALLS		
Main Wall	Long slanting gobelin	White
Gable wall	Tent	White

BASE OF HOUSE	Cashmere	DMC 3013, Anchor 853

WINDOWS		
Frames	Laid threads	Anchor 293
Upper panes	Upright cross	Anchor 122, DMC 844
Bars	Laid threads	DMC 293
Lower panes	Hungarian	Anchor 122, DMC 844

PORCH		
Roof	Tent	DMC 642, 844
Walls	Tent	White
Shadow	Tent	DMC 451

STEPS	Slanting gobelin	Anchor 853

DOOR	Slanting gobelin	DMC 502

STONE MANOR

This small manor house, worked by Janet Davies, is built of Ham stone, a particularly lovely golden limestone found in Somerset. Montacute House, the Elizabethan house belonging to the National Trust – in which the famous Goodhart Collection of samplers is displayed – and the village surrounding it, are built in this stone. Our manor has the colours of a newly built house but this stone weathers to richer and more sombre shades of gold.

Start by working the frame and surround of the door in slanting gobelin and then add the portico in laid threads. Now work the dressed edging and the dividing stone course in slanting gobelin. Outline the roof and work the coping in tent stitch and oblique gobelin and the cornice at its base in oblique gobelin. Fill the roof with cashmere in various shades. The chimneys are created with blocks

of slanting gobelin with divisions of overlaid thread. Now you can work the surrounds of the top windows in oblique gobelin and those of the bottom windows in slanting gobelin. Fill them with blocks of cashmere stitch for the panes and overlay threads for the frames and window bars. The round window is worked in back stitch, filled with large-scale slanting gobelin and the bars are made with overlaid threads. The decorative panel below this window is a single rococo stitch surrounded by tent stitch. Fill the walls with cashmere stitch. The door consists of blocks of slanting gobelin, changing\scale and direction for emphasis (refer to the photograph for guidance). The steps are created with rows of slanting gobelin laying long threads in dark gold to create the divisions. The finishing touch is provided by the railings which are overlaid threads in black.

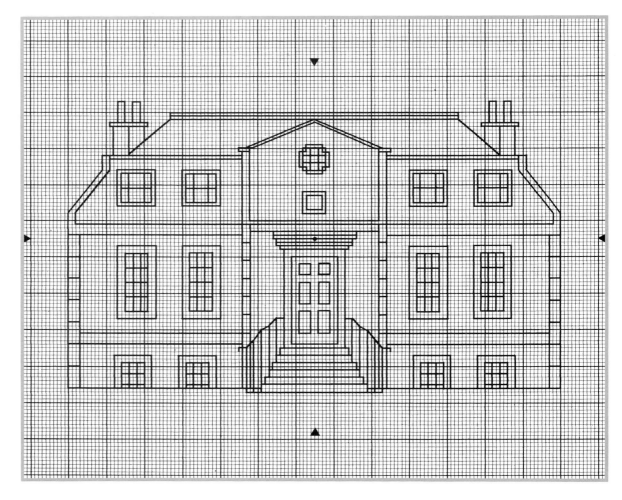

STONE MANOR
Key to colours and stitches

CHIMNEYS	Slanting gobelin and laid threads	Anchor 888	WINDOWS Surrounds	Oblique and slanting gobelin	
ROOF				and back stitch	DMC 644
Ridge	Oblique gobelin and tent	DMC 642	Panes	Cashmere	DMC 413
Main roof	Cashmere	Anchor 8581, DMC 642, 647, 3011, 3023	Frames and bars	Overlaid threads	White
			DECORATIVE PANEL	Rococo and tent	Anchor 888
			DOOR		
			Main panels	Slanting gobelin	White
WALLS			Surround	Slanting gobelin	DMC 642
Main area	Cashmere	Anchor 874, 887, DMC 834	Portico	Laid threads	DMC 644
			STEPS	Slanting gobelin	DMC 644
Edging and stone course	Slanting gobelin	DMC 644	Divisions	Laid threads	Anchor 888
			RAILINGS	Laid threads	Black

VICTORIAN LODGE

This lodge house with its curved barge boards and windows and its roof of ogee-shaped tiles is an example of Victorian Gothic architecture. Many such lodges are scattered about the country. The large house with the grounds it once guarded may have disappeared and the lodge could now be surrounded by modern building development. It is difficult to specify a particular area from which these lodges originated as they were usually built to complement and match a main house, the building materials of which were very often imported from elsewhere.

Start by outlining the roof of the porch and house in tent stitch. Work the barge boards in Florentine stitch following the angle of the roof. Now use the same technique with the stone window surrounds and the windows, overlaying the two shades of turquoise with frames and window bars in black, and work the sills in slanting gobelin. The dressed stonework edging the walls and doors can now be worked in blocks of slanting gobelin. The roof on the main gable is edged with oblique gobelin stitches which should follow its angle. Outline the chimney stacks in tent stitch and fill with brick stitch. Each pot is a single cashmere stitch. Fill the roof with Hungarian stitch in different shades of purple and blue and the walls in green tent stitch. The door is worked in rows of slanting gobelin, the hinges overlaid in black thread and the knob is a small French knot.

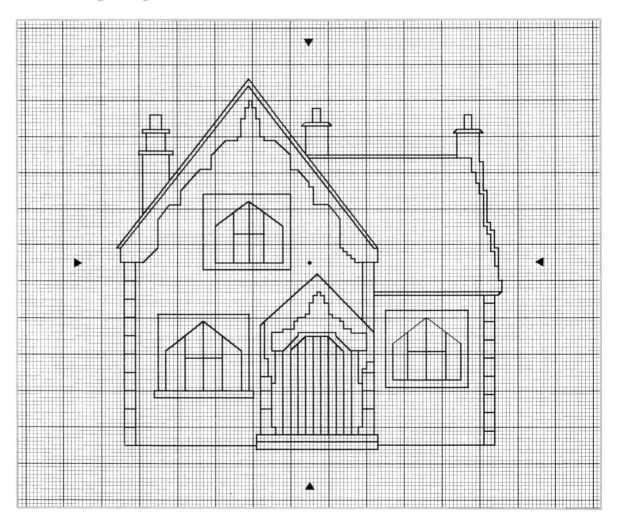

VICTORIAN LODGE
Key to colours and stitches

CHIMNEYS			WINDOWS		
Pots	Cashmere	DMC 644	Stonework surround	Florentine	
Edging	Oblique gobelin	DMC 644		and slanting	
Stacks	Brick	DMC 922,		gobelin	DMC 644
		3772	Panes	Florentine	Anchor 922,
					DMC 926
ROOF			Frames, bars and lattice	Laid threads	DMC 844
Gable	Oblique gobelin	DMC 3740			
Barge boarding	Florentine	White	PORCH		
Main roof	Hungarian	DMC 327,	Roof	Oblique gobelin	DMC 3740
		3740, 3041,	Barge boarding	Florentine	White
		Anchor 122	Stone edging	Cashmere	DMC 642
Guttering and ridge	Oblique gobelin		Walls	Slanting gobelin	Anchor 392
	and tent	Anchor 873			
			DOOR	Slanting gobelin	White
MAIN WALLS	Tent	Anchor 858	Hinges	Overlaid thread	DMC 844
			STEPS	Slanting gobelin	DMC 644

OLD POST OFFICE

This tiny cottage with its bay window was based on one seen in Surrey. It is half timbered with brick-nogging between its beams and a roof of hand-made clay tiles, all weathered to mellow shades of terracotta. The lower half of the cottage is constructed in pink sandstone. Its brick porch is smothered by a climbing rose. Both roof tiles and the bricks of the upper part of the house have been worked in space-dyed thread which captures their subtle colouring.

Start by outlining the shape of the main roof and the gable of the dormer window in tent stitch. If you want to add the roses and shrubs to your post office, these must be worked before the walls. Work the beams in slanting gobelin and the barge boarding of the dormer in laid threads. The chimney stack is outlined with tent stitch and filled with pattern darning, the chimney is a cushion stitch. Work the window frames and door in slanting and oblique gobelin and laid threads. The bay window has oblique gobelin and laid threads to suggest its side window panes and bars, those of the main window and the door are cushion stitch worked in different directions, its window bars are overlaid threads. Fill the dormer window in slanting gobelin and overlaid threads. The porch walls are created with brick stitch and the lower house walls are blocks of irregular slanting gobelin with bare canvas left to represent mortar. You can now work the roof tiles in cashmere stitch and the guttering in oblique gobelin and laid threads. Next work the brick-nogging; to do this stitch slanting gobelin in two directions with spaces between. The post box is in tent stitch with overlaid threads to suggest details.

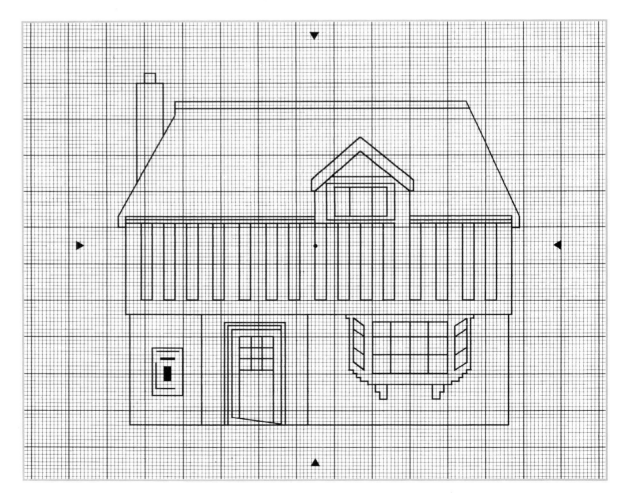

GEORGIAN HOUSE
Key to colours and stitches

CHIMNEYS	Brick	DMC 356	PORTICO		
Edge	Slanting gobelin	Anchor 398	Pillars	Laid threads and straight gobelin	Anchor 398, DMC 317
ROOF					
Ridge	Oblique gobelin	DMC 356	Pediment	Straight gobelin	Anchor 398
Guttering	Slanting gobelin	White			
Main roof	Cashmere	Anchor 849, DMC 926	DOOR	Tent and slanting gobelin	White, DMC 562
WALLS	Cashmere	DMC 356, 3778, Anchor 884, 5975	STEPS	Slanting and straight gobelin	DMC 647
WINDOWS					
Frames	Slanting gobelin and tent	White			
Panes	Cashmere	Anchor 922			
Bars	Laid threads	White			

TOLL HOUSE

The roof of this house worked by June Rees was glimpsed over a wall, the rest is imaginary but it is typical of the little toll houses built alongside roads and bridges, where money was collected for the right of passage. Though they are extremely attractive to look at, their odd shape, and unusual decorative detailing, must have made them very awkward to live in. This one has pointed Gothic windows with leaded lights. These have been worked in back stitch and laid thread as it would be difficult to show such detail in any other way.

Start by outlining the roof in tent stitch and work the coping stones in straight gobelin following the angle of the rest of the roof. Next work the chimney stack in slanting gobelin stitch and pattern darning, and the pot in cushion stitch. Work the windows in

back stitch and laid threads. The dressed stonework edging comprises blocks of slanting gobelin outlined in laid threads, and the base of the house and upper window sill are created with slanting gobelin. The decorative frieze is worked in cross stitch and the motif over the lower windows in rococo stitch. The shape of the door is formed by working the top and the stonework above in straight gobelin, and the door frame and panels in slanting gobelin. The fanlight is shaped with straight gobelin and filled together with the lattice panes of the door with laid threads. The roof can now be filled with straight and diagonal mosaic stitch. The guttering is formed with oblique gobelin and the barge boarding is created by laying long threads at the same angle as the guttering. The walls are filled with tent stitch.

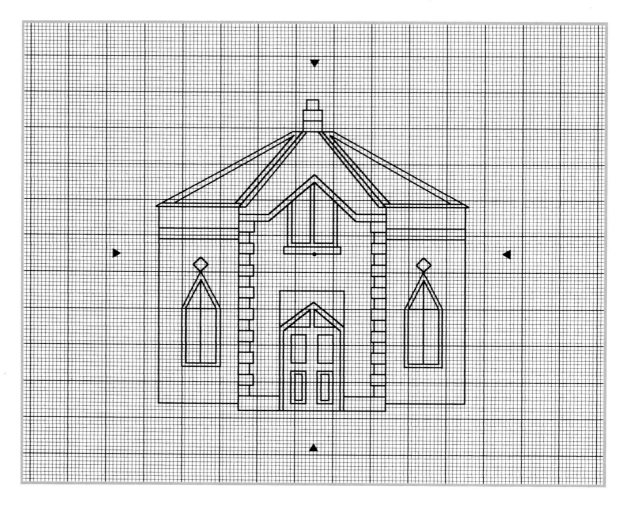

COTSWOLD COTTAGE
Key to colours and stitches

CHIMNEYS	Slanting gobelin	DMC 833
ROOF		
Main roof	Cashmere	DMC 611, 3045, Anchor 888
Roof of dormers	Cross	DMC 640
WALLS		
Stone quoins	Cashmere and cushion	DMC 833, Anchor 888
Main wall	Tent	DMC 833
WINDOWS		
Frames	Tent	White
Panes	Cashmere	DMC 318, 413
Bars	Laid thread	White
Sills	Oblique gobelin	Anchor 888

PORCH		
Roof, infill and shadow	Tent	White, DMC 640, 3045
DOOR		
Frame	Slanting gobelin	White
Panels	Slanting gobelin	White
Surround	Tent	White
Step	Slanting gobelin	Anchor 888
CONSERVATORY		
Frame	Tent, oblique and slanting gobelin and laid thread	DMC 3752

CHAPTER FIVE

Designing Your Own House

A HOUSE is one of the simplest objects to draw. It is often the first picture drawn at play school – a box-like house with path and gate, maybe with the sun overhead and perhaps with a matchstick figure in the foreground representing one of the family. We should not be put off when we come to draft a house chart – we have done it before! The only difference is that this time we need to draw our house on graph paper.

Many of the houses in this book are based on the simple shapes of traditional buildings. British vernacular architecture is rich in styles and building materials, and it is challenging to try to capture these different shapes and textures in stitchery. However, these same stitching techniques can be used to portray houses from many different countries, it is just a matter of adapting the ideas shown here to suit your own locality. For example, the method used on the weather-boarding of the Kent cottage (see page 54) can be used for wooden houses in different parts of the world, from North America to Australia.

favourite things – flowers, birds, animals – and adding an appropriate quotation or a descriptive verse. It may seem like a tall order to stitch a dream, but this may well be the only chance of ownership.

To chart an imaginary house, start by drawing a rectangle, 90 squares high by 100 squares wide, on a piece of graph paper. Use this as a basic size though it can be altered if necessary. If the house you dream of is squarer, then draw the rectangle 100 squares high by 100 squares wide. The basic shape can now be divided up by drawing in the roof line and its angle, then the doors, windows and chimneys. I have included a selection of these from which you can choose, but you may have your own ideas. Unlike an architect, you do not have to worry whether your dream house is comfortable or practical to live in – it just has to look good. Let your imagination take over.

Try to express your ideas within this basic frame. A little leeway is permissible but if you make your

BASIC HOUSE SHAPE

DRAWING A DREAM HOUSE

Many of us have a house which is caught in our imagination, either one we know and long to own or just a picture that we have seen somewhere that keeps recurring. Now we have the chance to turn this dream into a form of reality by embroidering such a house and embellishing it with all our

(Opposite) All six of these houses have been based on the basic house shape on page 78. This basic outline can be clearly seen in three of the houses opposite - the Kent cottage, the Welsh Border farmhouse and the Hampshire cottage - but the others have had the position of their windows and doors altered and their roof lines are very different, so the connection is not so apparent. Try placing tracing paper over the basic house chart and experiment by drawing a variety of shapes.

Weather-boarded cottage, Kent

Victorian Gothic lodge, Derbyshire

Toll house, Gwent

Farmhouse, Welsh Borders

Flint and brick cottage, Hampshire

Old Post Office, Surrey

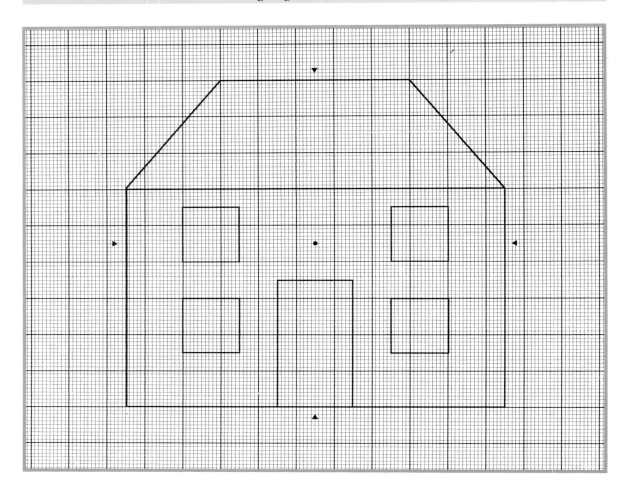

house much larger it will not fit the basic sampler plan, and if you make it much smaller there will not be enough squares on the graph paper to show the details that will make your house interesting, nor will you have room to use a variety of stitches.

Think of the smallest detail you want to include, as the way you decide to handle this will set the scale for the whole house. For example, the glazing bars on windows influence the appearance of windows dramatically, and these in turn give character to the house – so how you decide to stitch this tiny detail is important.

DRAWING A REAL HOUSE

Obviously, if you are portraying a particular house it has to resemble the real thing. Its proportions and colours have to be correct and any unique features have to be present so that the house is easily recognizable. However, this is an embroidery and artistic licence can be used. When it is finished it has to stand as a picture in its own right, to appeal to those seeing it now, or in the future, who do not know the real house.

Decide on the features of your house – those which will give it its character and make it distinctive – and allow enough room for them on your chart. To help you, use the 100 squares by 90 squares rectangle as a basic measurement (see above). The challenge is to capture the essence of the house and make a pleasing picture, but remain true to the medium you are working in.

Start by simply drawing your house straight on to graph paper, using the same method as drawing a dream house described previously. If you do not feel confident to do this yourself, maybe a member of your family could do it for you? It is rather nice to involve the family, they will take more interest in your work and will appreciate the finished embroidery more if they have contributed to it.

A WELSH FARMHOUSE

This old Welsh farmhouse in the Vale of Glamorgan is the home of the Hurst family and here it is captured in midsummer when its garden borders brim with a wonderful array of cottage garden flowers. Melanie has used tent stitch for her house walls, window and door frames and filled their panes and panels with slanting gobelin. The roof is horizontal cashmere stitch in a variety of greys and the chimney stack is brick stitch with its pot worked in straight gobelin. The garden wall and the stonework edging the house walls is a mixture of cushion and cashmere stitch and the flowers are worked in French knots, eyelets, tent and laid threads using some space-dyed threads. The sky is worked in a variegated blue thread.

This picture shows the house's extension which has been converted from original stabling. This composition highlights the problem that all extensions can pose when you are trying to create a balanced picture. In real life, extensions are built to fill the maximum space available for practical living. But to produce a pleasing picture we must use artistic licence and either invent balance by adding extra trees and garden or by deciding to portray just the main part of the house.

It is always better to draw a facing view and not a side view which can lead you into difficulties with perspective and present problems when it comes to stitching. If you live in a new house or have had some alterations made to your home, you may still have the front elevation drawing needed by planning authorities. This can be a wonderful help as it offers no problems with perspective and can be either enlarged or reduced by photocopying to fit the basic measurement, of 100 by 90 squares, and then traced on to your graph paper.

It is helpful to use a photograph as the basis for your design. When you take a picture of your

Here is a selection of equipment needed to design your own sampler chart. As you can see, I made a tracing directly from a photograph of the terraced house opposite, then transferred it to graph paper. This is a time-consuming procedure but worth the trouble if you have a complicated house to chart.

Mary Jenkins '89

LOUISE'S HOUSE
*This was a wedding present for my friends Louise
and Paul Rutledge and features their first house.
The house is a typical Victorian terraced home,
and there are thousands similar to this one all
over the country.*

'WINDERMERE' (Overleaf)
*This is a much loved family home with a beautiful
garden. It is very modern in comparison to the other
houses in this book. Truda Theodore has worked the
house, trees and shrubs in a variety of textured
stitches but the border, which includes all her
favourite flowers, is worked in tent stitch.*

house, remember to include the chimneys. It can sometimes be difficult to fit the whole house into one shot, especially if it is situated on a narrow or busy road so that you cannot stand far enough away. If this is the case take several photographs of different parts of the house and stick them together. You could try taking the picture from your opposite neighbour's house. Their upstairs front window may have the perfect view. Or it may be easier to take a photo of a house similar to your own and adapt it.

You can enlarge your photograph to match the suggested basic measurement of approximately 100 square by 90 squares on your graph paper. The photocopy need not be in colour and it need not be the best quality. You can now place your graph paper over the enlarged copy and trace the outlines of the main parts of the house. To make this easier stick the copy against a window with masking tape, then place your graph paper over it. Mark the roof line first, then the other important measurements such as the placement of windows and doors. An alternative method is to place a light underneath a glass table and stick the copy on the glass top and trace it there. You can add details when you remove your drawing from the window or tabletop. When you are satisfied that the drawing resembles your house, all the lines can be squared off.

SOME PROBLEMS SOLVED

Many houses have features that are difficult to portray when working in the medium of counted thread. Here are a few difficult areas with suggestions on how to deal with them.

Extensions

Front and side extensions cause enormous problems with perspective and can also make the picture look unbalanced. I recommend screening them out by charting only part of the house, isolating it within a frame.

If the extension to your home is particularly important to you, chart it separately. The two, original house and extension, could stand side by side within the same picture.

Semi-detached houses

There are two ways of tackling this type of house either work both the houses in the same way, or work your house in detail and your neighbour's in less detail or just in outline. Bear in mind that if you ignore the attached house, or try covering it by a tree, it can look rather contrived and unbalanced.

Curves and circles

Curves can be worked only if a sufficient number of threads have been allocated for them. If you try to work a very small circle, for example, it will appear quite angular. I have embroidered a small decorative window on Rose Lodge (see page 18). In reality it would be a 'bull's eye' window but here it has slight angles and is not circular. This is where artistic licence must play its part.

Bay and bow windows

These windows are a dominant feature in many houses so a sufficient number of squares on the graph paper must be allocated to do them justice. As they are so important, the treatment of this type of window will set the scale for the house.

Sometimes it is necessary to lay threads instead of working individual stitches, as this can suggest shallow slopes where there is insufficient space to portray them any other way.

WINDOWS
The windows at the top of the opposite page are variations on a simple casement. The two central ones show the difference in size caused by either laying threads across the already stitched panes or by working them as a row of tent stitches, making the whole window appear relatively larger.

All the windows should have their glass worked in quite dark grey, blue or turquoise threads. The windows are the 'eyes' of a house, giving it its personality, so they must stand out sufficiently against all the other elements.

The most useful stitches for creating windows are tent and slanting gobelin stitches, together with laid threads, but others such as Hungarian or upright cross stitch can be used to give the effect of leaded lights and lattice panes, see the small Gothic dormer window on the opposite page.

ROOFS

The clock turret with weathervane has a roof of upright cross stitch, and the thatched roof is split gobelin with a chimney of diagonal cashmere. The Cotswold house has both chimney and roof worked in cashmere and slanting gobelin. The gabled house has a roof of twill and a chimney stack of brick stitch, the chimney is diagonal mosaic. The Scottish house roof is oblique gobelin worked in four colours to suggest lichen-covered tiles. Its turret is in cashmere with a roof of brick stitch. The row of cottages has a split gobelin thatch and a pantiled roof in long armed cross stitch; the clay tiled roof and all the chimneys are worked in cashmere.

86

DOORS

In working these doors Janet Davies has used slanting gobelin for the panels. This is a quick and effective way to stitch them. A well chosen shade for the door can do wonders for your house picture. If, however, you are portraying a real house, the door colour should be accurate, though you could brighten it up a little to give the whole picture extra zip. Quite vibrant shades have been used for some of these doors and they work well.

'ROSSIGNOL' (Overleaf)

These traditional-style mock Tudor houses became popular in the thirties and are still being built today. This attractive house is in North Wales and belongs to good friends of mine. This picture was a present for their silver wedding anniversary.

Rossignol
Ruthin

CHAPTER SIX

Gardens

Not all gardeners admire embroidery, but it certainly seems that most embroiderers love gardens. Flowers have been a dominant subject in needlework through the centuries, and there have been many excellent books written exploring and illustrating the seemingly inseparable link between embroidery and gardening.

Embroiderers obviously find great inspiration from flowers and gardens, but I prefer to stitch – there is no exhausting digging, planting and mulching. When embroidering a garden I am in control. I am the garden designer, but without any physical effort, and with no weather or soil conditions to worry me.

As embroiderers we can make all our favourite plants bloom at the same time. Just like the gardens at the Chelsea Flower Show, anything goes in our dream garden. Or we can restrict ourselves to the seasons – design a spring garden which lends itself well to canvas embroidery. Spring flowers tend to be stiffer in form which makes them easy to capture. High summer gives tremendous scope. All the favourites, from roses to delphiniums, bloom then. Late summer and autumn have more flamboyant colouring – think of sunflowers, dahlias and Virginia creeper. Winter has a delicate beauty which, with the exception of the Christmas period, is often neglected. The shape and structure of plants and trees can be shown and berries can decorate the evergreens.

It is a pleasant task to browse through gardening books, studying pictures of gardens with magnificent flower borders. Many magazines have wonderful photographs which you can cut out and use to make a design on paper. This will give you a basic plan from which to work.

SOME RULES TO GUIDE YOU

When portraying flowers and shrubs two things are important. First choose just the right colour for the flowers; also try to capture the shape and drape of the plant itself. Does it stand up straight or does it flop over in a certain position when growing alongside others? If you get these elements right, your plants will be recognizable with the minimum of stitching.

When selecting flowers for a border there must be a balance of colour as well as shape. Do not position all your tall flowers or all your blue ones on one side. The colours in your picture garden should be carried through to the rest of the embroidery. Do not suddenly introduce a new colour, it may jar. If you want delphiniums make sure you include their colours in the selection you make at the planning stage.

DIFFERING SCALES

You may want to work flowers on several scales. The gardens behind houses should appear distant (see the Weather-boarded Cottage on page 54), borders, in the middle distance, and flowers in the foreground (see Lavender Cottage on page 94) should be comparatively large.

SAMPLER FOR JUNE (Opposite)
This was made for a special birthday. The imaginary house is just a focus for the surrounding garden. The family schnauzer, Otto, has since died but he is remembered with affection.

My garden is well planted

with flowers everywhere

Distant flowers should be worked in very pale colours. As you have only a small number of stitches with which to suggest a particular plant, use tent stitch. Any other stitch may draw the eye to the area, and this is not the intention. You can use some texture for flowers in the middle distance but keep to the smaller stitches, reserve the larger ones, such as eyelets, for the flowers in the foreground.

Generally, small-scale stitches such as upright cross, diagonal mosaic and basic tent stitch work best. French knots can be worked tightly or loosely to suggest anything from berries to roses.

There is advice on the choice of threads for stitching gardens in Chapter Two with guidance on the potential of space-dyed and variegated threads for portraying foliage and flowers.

STEP-BY-STEP FLOWERS

These examples show how your favourite flowers can be built up gradually from a foundation of threads. The shape and density of a plant and the way it stands, combined with the exact colour of foliage and flowers, should make it immediately recognizable. Use a coloured photograph as a reference – do not rely on your memory.

Border plants should have a base of soft-coloured greens and greys, working from dark up to light. Finally, add the brighter colours required by your plant. Use only one thread of each shade in your needle to give a lighter, airier impression for both foliage and flowers.

Stitch the basic shape of the plant in your darkest thread, add another two layers of progressively lighter thread. Finally add the flower colours bringing the plant to life.

(Opposite) More flowers and a border of perennials. They were chosen for their strong shape and identifiable colours.

As climbing plants are denser, work with three threads in your needle to build up the shape. Space-dyed threads are excellent for this purpose as they immediately introduce a variety of greens from one skein. The flowers, such as roses, can then be added, using French knots, eyelets or cross stitches.

LAVENDER COTTAGE (Opposite)
This sampler was worked on linen (25 threads per inch). As well as a flower border by the cottage, I have included larger-scale flowers in the foreground. The foxgloves have been worked with a variegated pink thread and the lavender in variegated purple. The daisies and the hollyhocks are worked in eyelets with centres of tent stitch and French knots. The lavender's flowers, the lettuces and the bees are also worked with French knots.

GARDEN FEATURES (Above)
Here are a few stitched ideas for objects that can be found in gardens. With a wide variety and choice of materials available there is added scope for using alternative stitches to suggest textures. For example, I have used rococo for the basket but upright cross or tent stitch worked over alternate threads could be used instead. However, the majority of the stitches are fairly simple, mostly tent, brick, slanting and straight gobelin and laid threads.

A field, then cottages with trees,
and last The distant hills + sky

STANDARDS AND TOPIARY (Opposite)
The formal shape of standards and topiary can be shown in a variety of stitches. Here I have used upright cross, straight and diagonal mosaic, diagonal cashmere, French knot, oblong cross and leaf stitch together with tent and slanting and encroaching gobelin for the pots. The centre of the sunflower provides yet another use for highly textured rococo stitch. Many of the threads used are space-dyed, giving more life and interest to what would otherwise be flat blocks of colour.

TREES AND SHRUBS (Above)
I have taken liberties with the seasons here as the shrubs and trees would not flower at the same time. The basic stitches are tent and diagonal mosaic with straight gobelin, laid threads, French knots and eyelets used to represent flowers, foliage and branches, while the tree trunk in the foreground is in encroaching gobelin. The embroidery is enclosed by a space-dyed cord which is couched to the canvas. The quotation is from Thomas Hardy's poem 'Domicilium'.

CHAPTER SEVEN

Animals

Through the centuries animals have been second only to flowers as a favourite subject of the embroiderer.

From the Bayeux Tapestry of the eleventh century, through to the embroideries of the fifteenth century, heraldic beasts and stylized symbolic animals were sewn. When pattern books were first printed in the sixteenth century, animals were copied directly from them on the same scale as the book illustration. So if a bird or a moth in the pattern book was the same size as a lion, then this was how it appeared on the embroidery. These books contained many strange beasts which were copied even though the stitcher had no first-hand knowledge of them, sometimes with humorous results. This practice of copying from pattern books continued through to the seventeenth century. The themes embroidered on the wonderful caskets, mirror frames and elaborate cushions, as well as their individual details, were all taken from books and drawn for the embroiderers by professional draftsmen. The animals, insects and flowers were exact copies, but the human figures, though based on engravings, were given contemporary costumes. Sewn in stumpwork, beadwork and canvaswork, they have a naïve and fairytale quality.

Embroidery has always echoed the contemporary tastes in home furnishings, and in the elegant era of the eighteenth century when the Oriental influence was at its height, the exotic birds, insects and animals sewn were those seen on the chintzes and porcelain imported from the East. It was not until the Victorian era that domestic animals became so important on embroideries. The Queen loved her pets and stitched their likeness, and so it seemed did thousands of her subjects, and these very same patterns are still being reproduced today.

Looking back through centuries of embroidered animals today's embroiderer should take comfort from the fact that she cannot go too far wrong. Naïve or skilful, animal embroideries appeared in great variety. If beautifully sewn they are magnificent, if badly sewn they are endearing. This should give us confidence in tackling the representation of our pets and other animals in our own samplers.

You will find many animals in various poses on the samplers in this book, but as you may wish to chart and embroider your own pet the following general guidelines may help you.

Before you start, decide where you want your pet to be positioned on your sampler. If you want your pet in the foreground of the picture allow yourself a relatively large number of squares on your graph paper; 35 by 35 squares is usually a sufficient number to chart a dog, depending on its pose. Use less for a cat, about 30 by 30 squares. This measurement should be helpful as a guide to assessing the space needed for other animals. A tortoise or rabbit, would need significantly fewer squares.

You could base your own cat on one I have worked on pages 102 and 103, all you need to do is to simply change its colour and markings. If your own breed of dog is not included on pages 100 and 101, you may need to start from scratch. If you have a suitable photograph of your pet you can trace it on to fine-squared graph paper (with 1, 5 and 10 mm divisions). Then to make it easier when you come to sew, copy the small chart on to the larger graph paper which you are using for the main sampler chart.

Children's books, greetings cards and advertisements are all very good sources for finding animal pictures. They are usually a suitable size to trace and clearly drawn, with a minimum of fussy detail, which make them ideal for charting. If they are not quite the right size to match the measurements suggested above, you can reduce or enlarge them using a photocopier and then trace them on to your graph paper.

WOODLAND CRESCENT
Our first house. Although we no longer live there this sampler provides us with a lasting reminder of our old home, together with the much-loved animals who shared it with us for a while. The embroidery design also features our flower and birth signs and symbols of our work.

DOGS

Dogs come in many more shapes and sizes than cats making them quite a challenge to stitch. It is essential to capture the essence and the variations of each kind as these differences mean everything to owners who often have great breed loyalty.

Practically all cats are beautiful, but this is not always so with dogs. Some are rather odd-looking, but this may simply be the characteristic of the breed. The knack is to catch the look and make it endearing in as few stitches as possible. The main thing to do is to choose the right colour combination, to place the eyes correctly and, of course, to catch the pose.

Although animals may be a major element of your sampler, only a limited amount of space is available for them on the canvas. If you use too much it will upset the balance of the whole sampler. A large dog will require enough space to allow you to portray the breed and make it easily recognizable. It depends how many squares are needed to get the outline right. Because there is a limited amount of space in which to work, I restrict myself to tent stitch even when depicting long-haired and shaggy dogs. It is easy to use too many stitches and end up with a rather messy concoction that does not resemble your particular pet. However, I do sometimes overlay the tent stitch with longer threads to suggest shagginess. The Yorkshire terrier (opposite) and the schnauzer on page 91 (June's Sampler) both have long threads around the face, but I keep this to a minimum to get the effect.

Fortunately libraries are full of books on dogs and the majority of breeds are included. I find those with drawn illustrations rather than photographs are easier to base a design on. There is so much choice that you can normally find an illustration in the scale you require, which also resembles your dog. This can then be traced on to graph paper giving you a basis for an originally designed chart.

where the Dog is

Border, Welsh & Yorkshire
Terriers

Golden
Labrador
& Puppy

Cavalier
King
Charles
Spaniel

Longhaired Dachsnund

Pug

West Highland Terrier

Old
English
Sheepdog

Pembrokeshire
Corgi

CATS

Cats are natural and unselfconscious models that have a gift for posing which appears instinctive yet deliberate. They also have the knack of choosing the perfect setting and make themselves comfortable whatever their surroundings. The ability of cats to dispose themselves attractively has inspired many artists, and they have become popular subjects on cards and calendars. We can now draw on this ready source of research material.

Although devoted owners believe that their cat is unique, most cats are similar in shape, so choose a particular position for your cat and only the colouring will need to be changed to resemble your pet.

Your picture will be more interesting if your cat appears to be following its own pursuits. It can be studying a butterfly, watching birds overhead, or leading the way into the house.

The markings of your cat should determine the choice of pattern scale. If your cat is black, its identity can be depicted easily on a small scale, rather than using a large dense mass of black. Other one-coloured cats can also be worked on a small scale, but they will not stand out as strongly of course. To make them distinctive, put them on a contrasting background colour or outline them in a darker shade.

It is better to portray cats with complicated markings on a larger scale. If they are worked too small, the different colours will merge together and become an unidentifiable blob. So if you have more than one cat to portray on your sampler, always keep the tabby for the foreground, the white cat for the middle ground and the black cat in the distance.

When stitching a cat outline the figure, first with tent stitch then fill in the head. It is important to get the angle of the ears and the spacing of the features correct. Getting these right will give you the confidence to proceed with the rest.

It is best to use mainly tent stitch because you are aiming to achieve simple lines and detail. Work this basic stitch so that it slopes in both directions to indicate the angle of the ears, back and tail. Study the pictures opposite to see where I have done this. As you have only a limited number of stitches in which to capture the characteristics of your cat, you must use every one to full effect. Tiny French knots or cross stitches can be used for eyes and nose; back stitches are suitable for mouths and outlining.

they are a laugh,

cuddle,

all of the time

some of the time.

CHAPTER EIGHT

Lettering: Verses and Numbers

LETTERING is the Cinderella of sampler design. It is so often tagged on as an afterthought and not considered enough at the design stage. I know from experience that students take enormous care designing their house and garden, then fly to the nearest cross-stitch publication to find a verse which has already been charted. They seem to run out of ideas at this point and will clutch at anything, even if it is quite unsuitable. If you consider lettering as a major element and think it through carefully at the planning stage of your sampler you will avoid this particular pitfall.

On old samplers, lettering was a minefield of mistakes, almost as bad as borders but not quite so obvious. In those days the stitchers of samplers were younger and less literate than we are today, and the lettering was all part of their learning. It was a schoolroom exercise chosen by the teacher. The mistakes made then, now add interest to their samplers and are often a cause of amusement.

The lettering of the verse you choose and the numbers used with it are important ingredients of your sampler. It is worth taking time and trouble to work out an appropriate size and style. It has to be in keeping with the whole design and must harmonize with the other main elements – the house and garden.

Consider how important your lettering is, what information you want it to impart and how it will reflect your personality and the times in which you live. If the sampler is for a special occasion, the best way to record this has to be carefully planned.

Write the wording on paper and consider what arrangement would look best. Maybe some of the lettering should be large and some much smaller. For example, if you are portraying your own house, featuring your pets, the name of the house could have large elaborate lettering in cross stitch, and the area or town in which you live could be worked in smaller cross-stitch letters. The names of your pets might be depicted in much smaller back-stitched lettering.

HELPFUL TIPS

1 Cross-stitch lettering and numbers take up more space than that worked in back stitch. Bear this in mind if you have limited space or a very long verse.

2 Darker coloured threads make more impact, particularly with back stitch. I use dark blue, red, green and grey for cross stitch and reserve black for back stitch.

3 Lettering looks more interesting if it is on several scales. Take some time and trouble selecting sizes and styles that complement each other.

(Opposite) I have adapted the border, alphabet and sunflowers in this little sampler from designs which are widely available, but all the other ingredients, including my tabby cat Poppy, are my own design.

Sometimes you have to chart the whole verse to see if it fits the space adequately and if it suits the other elements of your sampler. Very often several attempts have to be made before it looks absolutely right.

CHOOSING A VERSE

Verses chosen for old samplers were often rather depressing. It would truly reflect the age in which we live if, instead of copying, we used more up-to-date phrases and sayings. Think of your favourite quotation, and use that, or perhaps use a poem learned at school, or one that has special memories or significance to you and your family. You can always change the wording of an existing poem, for example S. Siddons' version of Shakespeare which I used on my Woodland Crescent sampler on page 99. Verses of popular songs certainly reflect the age

of the sampler, and can of course be short, catchy and sometimes humorous.

'I can see clearly now the rain has gone,
There are no obstacles in my way
Gone are the dark clouds that had me down
It's a bright, bright sunshiny day'

This verse from a song written by Johnny Nash in 1972 would be most suitable on a sampler.

If a favourite poem or verse of a song is too long, adapt it and just drop some of the lines. Browse through books of poems and quotations, and keep your ears open; if something someone says appeals to you, jot it down for use on future samplers.

There follows a selection of charts of lettering and numbers which have been used on many of the samplers in this book. You will find embroidery books are a good source of other styles, giving you unlimited choice.

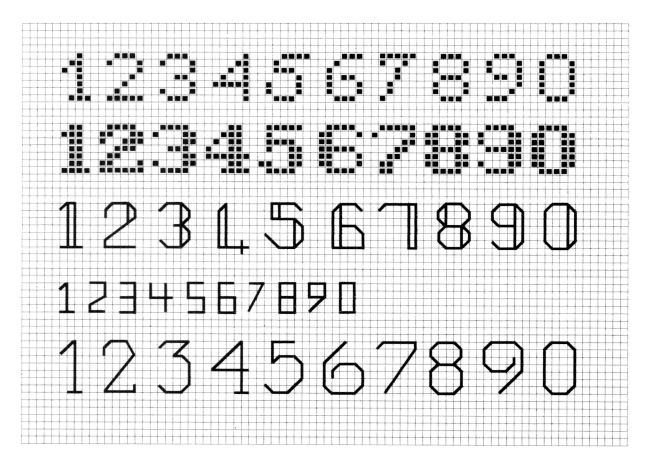

ABCDEFGHIJKLMN
OPQRSTUVWXYZ

ABCDEFGHI
JKLMNOPQR
STUVWXYZ

ABCDEFGHI
KLMNOPQR
STUVWXYZ

abcdefghijklm
nopqrstuvwxyz

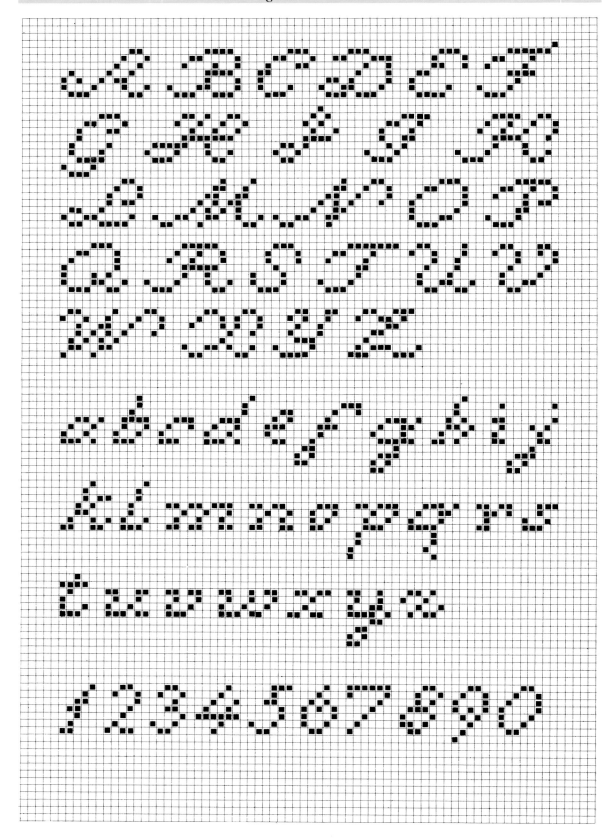

ABCDEFGHIJKLMNOPQ
RSTUVWXYZ abcdefgh
ijklmnopqrstuvwxyz

ABCDEFGH
IJKLMNO
PQRSTUV
WXYZ

abcdefghij
klmnopqrs
tuvwxyz

EAST ANGLIAN COTTAGE
Jilly Meredith worked my design of an East Anglian cottage turning it into a personal tribute to her beloved cats. The pargetting, which is a feature on cottages in that area, is a panel of rococo stitch; the lawn and roof are worked in split gobelin; and the chimney stack and the path are pattern darning on two scales. Jilly designed her own border incorporating a favourite quotation worked in back stitch, within a crescent of flowers.

CHAPTER NINE

Borders

INSPIRATION for border designs are everywhere. Look around and you will find them on bedlinen, curtains, wallpaper, gift wrapping and stationery. Any of these design sources can be adapted for your purpose. They can be enlarged or reduced by photocopying, traced on to paper and squared off to form patterns for use on samplers.

By using contemporary source material you are recording the style and fashion popular in homes today, just as embroiderers did in earlier times.

WORKING A BORDER

The border patterns of old samplers were often drawn or traced on to the material and the outlines filled with free flowing embroidery, although the main part of the sampler was worked using a counted-thread technique. However, it is the counted-thread borders of arcaded strawberries, carnations and other stylized flowers that we usually associate with early samplers. These formal flower borders are still popular today because they offer the traditional look that we so admire.

You only have to study old samplers, especially the corners, to see that sewing borders has always been a problem area. They were very rarely worked correctly. Viewed through the mists of time we find such errors charming. But now, at a more mature age, we strive for perfection and are not happy with our work if we leave glaring mistakes. This is why we spend so much of our time unpicking and restitching our work.

In this chapter I hope to help you to avoid the pitfalls of crooked corners, and encourage you to update the look of your embroidery but still remain true to the tradition of the art. If you love old borders, rather than just copying them, why not add a flower with a special significance for you or your family? A fuchsia or a daffodil perhaps? Both these flowers have a definite shape which can be successfully interpreted in embroidery, and many others are also suitable for this purpose.

Whether you decide to work a formal or meandering border, draw each side on a separate strip of graph paper. These strips can then be placed around the border section of the basic sampler plan. Sketch in the foundation line of your proposed design first and add the details later. For example, if you are planning a floral border, draw in the main stem first from which flowers and leaves grow. Make it fit the space and negotiate the corners before adding details such as leaves and flowers. This rule also applies when you stitch. Many of us have completed a border to find that the corners do not meet. If you work the foundation line only and make a mistake, you only have to unpick one line. Do not work the flowers and leaves until you are sure that your foundation line meets perfectly at each corner. Keep checking as you stitch. On a ring or hoop frame you can tack in some guidelines to help you and on a plastic frame you only have to run your needle across the canvas to make sure you are on target.

To avoid any possibility of the corners not meeting, design a border that has a separate corner piece. If there is a break between the corner piece and the side border, adjustments can be made to cope with small errors if they do occur, giving you some leeway.

FLOWER BORDERS: STEP-BY-STEP

1 Working first in pencil, draw the foundation line of your border on strips of graph paper.
2 Square it off by marking each stitch you intend to make with a cross. Follow the line as closely as you can.
3 Decide on the type of flower you would like to stitch and draw or trace it on a separate piece of graph paper. You can repeat a single flower, make slight changes, or use a mirror image. The easiest way to obtain a mirror image is to outline the chosen flower or motif with a very dark pen so that when you turn the paper over the outline shows on the reverse – ink over this to make it clearer for tracing.

Place another sheet of graph paper over the image and trace it, this gives you the reverse form. This method can be used for any motif, animal or figure, and is much easier than using a mirror. When you have drawn your flowers, square them off by overlaying the drawn outline with crosses to represent stitches, following the curves as closely as you can, just as you did with your foundation line.
4 When you have decided on your flower and its variations, make copies of them and position them around your border, on or near the foundation line.
5 Use the same method for the leaves or draw them directly on to the graph paper using the position of the flowers as a guide.
6 When you are satisfied with your design, ink over the outlines and colour in the leaves and flowers.

SINGLE FLOWER BORDER

A different effect can be achieved by scattering flowers around the main part of the sampler as shown on the Daisy Cottage sampler on page 26. The space between the flowers can be varied or extra flowers added, making this a very adaptable border for many samplers. All you have to do is to draw or trace a flower on to graph paper as described previously. You can reverse the flower for the other side of the border or you can use different flowers. Cut out each one and arrange them around the border area. When you are satisfied with the design, stick them in place.

OTHER TYPES OF BORDERS

LINES

One of the simplest borders for a sampler is created using lines of stitches in varying widths and density (see page 46). When selecting colours, place strands of thread directly from the skein in lines on the piece of work, this will give you an idea of how they will look when worked. Echo the colours already used in the sampler.

LATTICE AND TRELLIS

For a variation of the line border, work cross stitches between the lines, creating a lattice effect.

The trellis window pattern in the border of the Woodland Crescent sampler on page 99 was charted as a part of the overall design, and the areas around the windows were filled with widely-spaced rows of cross stitch. These windows allowed the inclusion of pets, symbols and personal motifs.

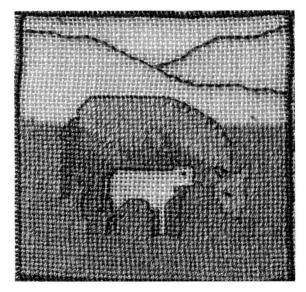

Detail of border from Woodland Crescent sampler.

DECORATIVE STITCHES

Many of the stitches featured in this book would make very attractive borders and some, such as diagonal mosaic or continuous cashmere, could be worked with minimal planning.

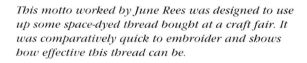

Florentine stitch too can be used to fill a border and if the pattern is worked sideways along the vertical edges, with a feature in each corner, the border will require minimal planning.

This motto worked by June Rees was designed to use up some space-dyed thread bought at a craft fair. It was comparatively quick to embroider and shows how effective this thread can be.

Corner detail of a diagonal mosaic stitch border.

Lettering can be employed to create an interesting border with scope for using larger or more elaborate lettering (see pages 88–89).

SPACE-DYED THREADS

These threads can make quick and effective borders which need the minimum of planning. I usually use the multicoloured skeins rather than the one-colour variety. On the samplers on pages 37 and 45 I have used these threads to work borders in slanting gobelin and Norwich stitch.

FABRIC

A fabric border can be very effective if the right material is chosen. Always take your embroidery with you when looking for a framing fabric and lay it on various bolts of material in the shop. Keep an open mind where colour is concerned and do not always go for a safe choice. Try different shades, colours and scales, as your embroidery may match a fabric that seems unsuitable at first.

CHAPTER TEN

Finishing Techniques

WHEN you have spent many hours planning, designing and stitching your sampler your finished embroidery deserves the utmost care and attention at this final stage. The following advice will help you to avoid any mishaps as you complete the cleaning and framing of your work.

PROTECTION AND CLEANING

It is important to protect the material while work is in progress. Linen is washable but if you saturate canvas it will lose its stiffness. Always cover your work when you put it down, even for a short time, to ensure it is kept clean and to avoid accidents. Store it in a bag or a cotton pillowcase. Get into the habit of putting it away if you are interrupted or at least cover it. It goes without saying that your hands should be clean at all times while you are handling your work.

If you have a spillage, blot up as much as you can with a clean towel and rinse the area immediately. A small amount of mild detergent (one suitable for washing wool) can be gently dabbed on stubborn

———————————

This sampler was inspired by a small painted box and the quotation is a Swiss proverb. Janet Davies has brought the design alive with stitchery.

stains but rinse it out as quickly as possible. If you prick your finger, a tiny amount of blood can be removed with your own saliva.

If you wash linen never rub, scrunch or screw up the material. Do not use harsh detergents and do not leave your work to soak. Remove the excess moisture by gently patting with a clean, dry towel. Leave it to dry naturally, away from any direct source of heat, on a flat surface on another clean, dry towel, which will support it and absorb the moisture.

If you really need to clean canvas to remove stains or dirt, after patting it dry with a clean towel put it back in its frame and hope that the dressing in it holds, it should if you are careful.

Textile experts recommend rinsing in distilled or purified water to avoid the chemicals in tap water. This pure water can be obtained from any pharmacy. How valuable is your work? If you consider it as a future heirloom then it is worth the extra time, trouble and expense involved to keep it clean.

If you have worked your sampler using the stitches and frames that I have suggested, there should not be much distortion. However, when it is finally removed from its frame there may be some creasing where the material has been held by the frame. To remove this, place your embroidery face down on a clean towel and iron the areas surrounding the stitchery. You can steam press through a lightweight cotton cloth if creases are persistent. Never iron the embroidered area as this will flatten all the texture.

FRAMING

You could frame your sampler yourself, perhaps with an old, attractive frame you already have, but as the frame is so important to the finished appearance of the sampler it does require skill and experience to choose one. Only professional framers have the range of products and the knowledge to advise you on the most suitable frame.

Take very great care in choosing your framer. I cannot emphasize this enough and speak from bitter experience having had a sampler ruined during framing. Make sure your chosen framer is used to working with textured embroideries as they are a very different medium to paintings and prints. For instance, glass should not touch the embroidery or your stitches will be flattened, so allowance must be made for this in the framing process.

I have found it invaluable to talk to the person who is actually going to do the work. Difficulties can be discussed and an expert opinion sought. Many outlets offering framing subcontract the work so that you do not have direct contact with the framer, which makes it much more difficult to put things right if they do go wrong. If you are not sure where to go in your area, ask the advice of other embroiderers, or an embroidery teacher. A local specialist shop may offer framing, but do not assume that because it is a needlework shop it will offer the best service. Always ask for an estimate and, if you are not satisfied, shop around. Some shops offer a 'preparation for framing' service, but this will be an additional cost. Check on the method to be used: my sampler was ruined by unsuitable glue seeping through to the front of the work. If you are not sure, it may be safer to prepare it yourself.

PREPARATION FOR FRAMING

I would recommend talking to the framer and choosing the frame before cutting the card on which you will mount the sampler. Then you can measure the lip of the frame (the small indentation where the frame will cover the work to be framed) and make allowance for this in the overall measurement. If you do not, the frame may cover some of your stitching making the sampler look cramped.

You should decide how much space you will need around your stitching, before you start. With a craft knife cut a piece of acid-free card to the required size. You can buy the card from art supply shops. Place your sampler over the card and secure it using map pins inserted into the sides of the card. These short pins with large heads will keep your sampler in place. Make sure that it is evenly positioned on the card by measuring the borders as you pin. Now you can lace your sampler using extra strong thread.

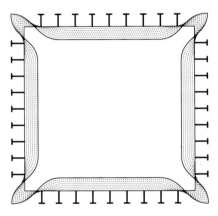

Pinning the fabric on to the board.

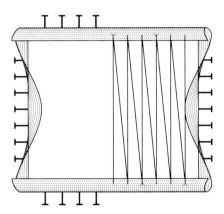

Lacing from the centre.

Start the lacing from the centre of each side of the work. Thread a long length of extra strong thread in a 22 tapestry needle, and secure it firmly at the centre of one side of your embroidery. Take it over to the centre of the opposite side and catch the edge by passing the needle through once. Return to the first side 1 inch further along. Repeat this process to the corner. Leave the thread loose.

Repeat this process all around the sampler, starting in the middle of each side. The ends of the threads can now be gently tightened until there is no slack and then fastened off. The pins can be removed and the corners tucked in and stitched down neatly.

I have never used non-reflective glass in a frame as I think it deadens the appearance of an embroidery and can cause the texture to appear distorted. It is probably best avoided.

WHERE TO HANG YOUR SAMPLER

When you have beautifully stitched and framed your sampler where should you hang this future heirloom?

All textiles are vulnerable and deteriorate in light from the moment they are made. Ideally they should be wrapped in acid-free tissue and kept in a dark drawer at a controlled temperature, they will then be in pristine condition in hundreds of years time. This is why textiles are not on show like other exhibits in museums. As we want to enjoy our samplers now, we must try to minimize the harmful effects that even normal living conditions can have on them. Do not hang your embroidery in a very light room, or over a fireplace or a radiator, or indeed anywhere that is very warm. Do not hang it on an exterior wall if you can avoid this as damp sometimes seeps through. Choose a dim area of your house, a landing that receives no direct light or a shaded corner of the room away from sunlight. If you have to hang your sampler on an exterior wall, make sure that the frame does not touch the wall by sticking a buffer on to the back of the frame.

Even people who should know better hang textiles in unsuitable places. Antique dealers hang old samplers in windows in full sunlight, and historical houses hang samplers and embroideries within window embrasures. Now you have sewn a sampler, and know the work involved and how precious they are, you are the custodian not only of your own but of all samplers.

Acknowledgements

So many people have helped me during my stitching career and in the production of this book. May I take this opportunity to thank them all.

Firstly, Anne Joyce late of the Embroiderers' Guild who, though she doesn't know it, started this whole process by spotting my work in an exhibition. My editor at David & Charles, Vivienne Wells, for giving me the chance and for focussing my ideas into a suitable form. To Cheryl Brown who succeeded Vivienne, Jane Trollope and Kay Ball for their help and guidance. Stephanie Aplin, friend and fellow patchworker who produced the charts and stitch diagrams, and Kevin Thomas and Tony Hadland of the National Museum of Wales for making the photography a painless and interesting process. To Jean Davies and Gill Thompson, both experienced teachers who helped me generously when I began teaching and who are still close and supportive. To Merrily Beams, my friend in California whose design was the very first sampler I sewed. To Brenda Keyes for chats on the phone. To Rambles, Stanwell Road, Penarth for lending equipment for photography. To the members of my local S.E. Wales E.G. Branch for all the jolly times we have had together. To my students; I probably learn more from them than they do from me. A very big thank you to my dear friends for stitching and lending their work – Jean Davies, Melanie Hurst, Jilly Meredith, Clare Probert, June Rees, Truda Theodore, Chris Minas, Beverly Morgan, Marjorie and Ivor Richards, Louise and Paul Rutledge and particularly Janet Davies, without whose help I would not have met my deadline. Lastly to all the animals who posed: some are gone but some are still very much with us particularly Frank, our black cat who appears constantly in my life and so in my work.

Thread Conversion Chart

For DMC, Anchor and Madeira stranded embroidery cotton (floss), and DMC and Anchor pearl cotton and coton à broder. If no equivalent is given, use the nearest colour available. The colour illustration of the project will help you.

DMC	ANCHOR	MADEIRA	DMC	ANCHOR	MADEIRA
White/neige	01	White	3011	0856	1607
727	0293	0110	3013	0843	1605
301	0349	2306	3022	0393	1903
310	Black	Black	3023	0392	1902
312	0148	1005	3024	0391	1901
317	0400	1714	3032	0903	2002
318	0398	1802	3041	0871	0806
327	0101	0805	3045	0943	2103
349	013	0212	3740	0873	0806
356	5975	0402	3747	0117	0907
370	0855	2111	3752	1032	1002
371	0855	2110	3772	1007	2310
407	0914	2310	3778	1013	0407
413	0400	1713	3787	0393	1811
414	0399	1801	793	0122	902
415	0398	1803	312	0148	1005
451	0399	1808	562	0211	1206
502	0877	1703	921	0338	402
611	0889	2107	814	0378	1912
612	0898	2108	ECRU	0387	ECRU
640	0393	1905	642	0392	1906
644	0391	1907	746	0590	–
727	0293	0110	3072	0847	1805
818	024	0502	927	0849	1708
823	0150	1008	613	0853	2109
833	0874	2203	3013	0854	2110
834	0945	2204	524	0858	1512
842	0376	1910	3740	0873	806
844	0401	1810	833	0874	2204
920	0339	0312	3064	0883	2312
922	0337	0310	301	0884	310
924	0851	1706	3046	0887	2206
926	0850	1707	3045	0888	2103
927	0848	1708	932	0920	1710
928	0847	1709	931	0921	1711
930	0922	1712	746	0926	1908
931	0921	1711	3022	8581	1812

Bibliography

A small selection of the many books I refer to for inspiration and instruction.

Erica Wilson's *Embroidery Book*, Faber 1973.

Patterns for Canvas Embroidery, Diana Jones, Batsford 1977.

Bargello Magic, Pauline Fischer and Anabel Lasker, J. M. Dent & Son 1972.

A New Look at Needlepoint, Carol Cheney Rome & Georgia French Devlin, George Allen & Unwin 1972.

The Complete Needlepoint Course, Anna Pearson, Century 1991.

Canvas Embroidery, Peggy Field and June Linsley, Merehurst 1990.

Embroidered Gardens, Thomasina Beck, Angus & Roberts 1979.

The Embroiderer's Garden, Thomasina Beck, David & Charles 1988.

The Embroiderer's Flowers, Thomasina Beck, David & Charles 1992.

Samplers & Tapestry Embroideries, Marcus B. Huish, Dover 1970, Batsford 1984.

Embroidery 1600–1700 at the Burrell Collection, Liz Arthur, John Murray 1995.

British Samplers, A Concise History, Jane Toller, Cultural Exhibitions with Phillimore 1980.

Catalogue of Welsh Folk Museum Samplers, F. G. Payne 1938.

Sampler Making 1540–1940, Joan Edwards, Bayford Books 1983.

Small Period Gardens, Roy Strong, Conran Octopus 1992.

Come into the Garden, Linda Benton & Jill Hollis, Ebury Press 1992.

The Best Plants for Your Garden, Anne Scott-James, Conran Octopus 1988.

Painted Gardens, English Watercolours 1850–1914, Penelope Hobhouse and Christopher Wood, Pavilion Books 1988.

Good Ideas for Your Garden, Reader's Digest 1995.

Your House the Outside View, John Prizeman, Hutchinson & Co 1975.

Old English Farmhouses, Bill Laws & Andrew Butler, Collins & Brown 1992.

Traditional Buildings of Britain, R. W. Brunskill, Victor Gollancz Ltd 1981.

Suppliers

Most of the equipment and materials for the samplers in this book can be obtained from stationers and shops selling embroidery supplies. If you have difficulty finding plastic frames or space-dyed threads they can be ordered directly from the manufacturers.

PLASTIC FRAMES
Universal Craft Frames, R & R Enterprises, 13 Frederick Road, Malvern Link, Worcestershire WR14 1RS. Telephone: 01684 563235.

SPACE-DYED THREADS
Stef Francis, Waverley, Higher Rocombe, Stokeinteignhead, Newton Abbot, Devon TQ12 4QL. Telephone: 01803 323004.

20th Century Yarns, The Red House, Guilsborough, Northants NN6 8PU. Telephone: 01604 740348.

Bits and Pieces, 4 Thorold Road, Bitterne Park, Southampton, Hants SO2 4JB. Telephone: 01703 553334.

Index